HOME

HOME
where reading and writing begin

Mary W. Hill

Heinemann
Portsmouth, N.H.

Heinemann
A division of Reed Elsevier Inc.
361 Hanover Street   Portsmouth, NH 03801-3912
Offices and agents throughout the world

© 1989, 1995 by Mary W. Hill
All rights reserved. No part of this book may be reproduced
in any form or by electronic or mechanical means, including
information storage and retrieval systems, without permission in writing from the publisher, except by a reviewer, who
may quote brief passages in a review.

The following have generously given permission to use material in this book:

Page 36: From *Seven Little Rabbits* by John Becker, illustrated
by Barbara Cooney. Text copyright © 1973 by John
Becker. Reprinted by permission of Walker and Company.

Page 38: From *It Didn't Frighten Me* by Janet L. Goss and Jerome C. Harste, illustrated by Steve Romney. Copyright ©
1985 by Willowisp Press. Reprinted by permission.

Library of Congress Cataloging-in-Publication Data

CIP information is available.

Cover design: Jenny Jensen Greenleaf
Printed in the United States of America
99 98 97 96 95 EB 5 4 3 2 1

to david and deborah

contents

Acknowledgments xi

1. Children and parents as learning partners 1

The Learning Partnership Includes Talking with and Listening to Others 3
The Learning Partnership Includes Working with and Observing Others 6
The Learning Partnership Includes Play and Family Recreation 8
An Invitation to Explore and Reflect 13

2. Environmental language is everywhere 17

The World of Reading That Children Want to Enter 17
The World of Writing That Children Want to Enter 25
An Invitation to Explore and Reflect 28

3. Reading books with children 31

Why Read Books to Children? 33
What Makes a Book Hold a Child's Interest? 36
Why Listen to Children Read? 42
Why Acquire a Personal Library? 47
How Can a Parent Find Time? 48
An Invitation to Explore and Reflect 50

4. Writing with children 53

Why Write with Children? 55
What to Look for in Children's Writing? 61
What to Provide in a Writing Place? 78
An Invitation to Explore and Reflect 79

5. Going to school: A continuation and expansion of the family partnership 83

Continuing the Family Partnership 83
Expanding the Family Partnership 87
An Invitation to Explore and Reflect 90

Starter list of read-aloud books and magazines 93

Bibliography 99

acknowledgments

The ideas found in this book began to take shape many years ago when the mother of one of my third-grade students asked what she could do at home to help her son David enjoy reading and writing. After we talked about the many things she was already doing and about some other things she might like to do, David's mother commented that she thought other parents would appreciate hearing about those things, too. As a result of this mother's comment, I developed a series of workshops intended to help parents rediscover—or at times even discover—the importance of the role they play in their children's language development and of the home as a literacy environment. Thus, I am indebted to Stacy Berman for suggesting that I talk with parents about the home being the place where reading and writing not only begin but also continue to develop.

I am also indebted to Carolyn Burke and Jerry Harste, who encouraged and helped me to conduct the first series of parent workshops and to write this book. Without their help I might never have begun this endeavor.

To Kathleen Scholl, Nancy Shanklin, and Virginia Woodward, I owe thanks for their responses to what I was writing. Their questions caused me to think more clearly about what I wanted to say. To Sharon Thomas, I owe thanks for the editing she did of this work. Her comments and suggestions were of immeasurable help. To Donna Brown, I owe thanks for the time she spent typing. Her willingness to do things at the last minute helped me make certain deadlines. And to Philippa Stratton, I owe thanks for the support she gave me while I wrote this book. Her suggestions from the point of view of both an editor and a parent helped me refine what I was writing.

Because this book could never have been written without the help of many children and parents, I owe a special thanks to all of them. To the children, I owe thanks for what they taught me about children knowing more about reading and writing than we've previously thought. To the parents, I owe thanks for what they taught me about the home being a literacy learning environment.

Lastly, I owe thanks to my family for supporting and encouraging me to write about home being the place

xii Acknowledgments

where reading and writing begin. In particular, I owe thanks to my son David, who has provided me with memories of his reading *The Owl and the Pussy Cat* and other favorite stories.

HOME

CHILDREN AND PARENTS AS LEARNING PARTNERS

Just as our parents were our first learning partners, we are our children's first learning partners.

Whenever another parent and I talk about experiences we've had in raising our children, the one thing we usually have in common is that neither of us went to school to learn how to be a parent. Instead, we've raised our children the best way we can and become their learning partners in the process. In the daily routine of family living we have helped them master crafts; learn family values; have a sense of their heritage; assume a role in society; and learn to talk, listen, read, and write. To do so, we've relied on our intuitive judgement, instincts, common sense and, in no small way, the skills we learned from our parents. Thus, just as our parents were our first learning partners, we are our children's first learning partners. Unfortunately, though, some of us do not recognize that fact, particularly as it relates to children's learning to read and write. Certainly the mother in the following story didn't realize that she was one of her daughter's first literacy-learning partners.

A few years ago I was invited to talk with a group of parents and teachers about the home as a literacy-learning environment and the role parents play in their children's learning to read and write. While I was sharing some thoughts, I could not help but observe a four-year-old child who had come to the meeting with her mother. In order to keep her daughter happy and out of mischief the mother had brought along a bag filled with small magnets, building blocks, picture books, papers, crayons, and pencils. While the adults talked, the four-year-old was engrossed in drawing, writing, looking at the picture books, and playing with the magnets and blocks. Periodically she would get up and walk around or show her mother something she had done, but for most of the time, she entertained herself by playing quietly near her mother.

While the little girl played, I remarked, "In order to realize that parents play an important role in their children's learning to read and write, all we need to do is look at all the teaching and learning of reading and writing that is going on here in front of us." Because many of the parents and teachers seemed unsure of what I was referring to, I called their attention to the bag of learning tools the mother had brought for her daughter to play with and to the work area she had selected, which

2 Children and parents as learning partners

was near enough for her to watch and to respond to her daughter. A rich learning environment including reading and writing—a combination of the child learning by using materials her mother had provided and the mother giving approval, encouragement, or instructions as her daughter needed or requested. Without question the mother had already established that she was one of her daughter's first partners in learning to read and write. Later I found out that because she considered herself to be illiterate, the mother, I'll call her Rose, was surprised to hear someone say that she was a partner in her daughter's literacy development.

I've often thought about the fact that Rose did not realize the important role she was already playing in her daughter's reading and writing development. And each time that I do, it's like looking into a mirror. I, too, never thought of myself as being involved in my son's learning to read and write. As a consequence, all of the family activities we engaged in—the puzzles we worked; the bedtime stories we read; the family outings we took; the special family events we prepared for; the gardening, cooking, cleaning, and redecorating we did; the conversations and even the disagreements we had—were unrecognized as important learning times that played an integral part in my son's learning to talk, listen, read, and write.

My experience tells me that Rose and I were not unusual in failing to recognize the literacy-learning partnership we share with our children. Learning to recognize that partnership is a first step in creating an even greater learning experience for them. As a means of discovering, or perhaps rediscovering, the role you play and the rich literacy-learning environment of your home, I invite you to take a mental walk with me. While on this walk we will explore some of the many things most of us do that support our children's literacy development. Because I will talk in chapter 2 about the environmental language, or print, that surrounds children, for now we'll focus primarily on the talking we do with children, the questions we ask of one another, the conversations children overhear, and the work and play we engage in—all activities that foster both oral and written language development.

The learning partnership includes talking with and listening to others

The learning partnership begins when we first cuddle and talk to newborn infants. As we hold them and tell them how happy we are that they have finally arrived, how cute they are, and how much they look like mommy or daddy, we help babies learn something about love, warmth, and security. At the same time we help them become aware of language that surrounds them.

Few, if any, people question whether or not they should talk to babies. They just do. Long before infants can produce words, most adults carry on conversations with them; usually these conversations center around the infant's well-being. We ask them if they are warm enough, if they are hungry, or if they are tired. To keep the conversation going, we make responses on their behalf. Eventually infants make their own responses by smiling or cooing, which prompt us to continue talking to them. By responding to what we say, infants seem to know that we will continue to talk to them. This cycle of mutual response is one of the ways children learn to communicate with others.

As infants smack their lips together and blow air or bubbles through their mouths, they soon discover they can make a number of sounds. By varying the pitch and tone of sounds, babies inform others of their needs. Eventually, those sounds become recognizable words.

Within a very short time after saying their first words, children become walking dictionaries and use language in interesting and unexpected ways. Several years ago Art Linkletter, in the book *Kids Say the Darndest Things* (1957), captured the essence of young children's use of language. Today Bill Keane does likewise in the cartoon *The Family Circus*. Parents who read his cartoons often remark that their children have made utterances similar to those of Buffy and Billy. Although Linkletter and Keane provide us with humor, they also provide us with

4 Children and parents as learning partners

insight into the fact that children have much knowledge of language at a young age.

One of the things children at a surprisingly young age learn is to ask "why." Although a child's persistence in asking this question exasperates most adults, each response helps children sort out additional information as well as rethink information they heard previously. When we watch instant replays on television or see a movie or television program more than once, we experience the same thing. With each repeated viewing, we have an opportunity to re-view what we just saw and to obtain more information. Intuitively, children seem to ask why as a means of re-viewing what they just heard and getting additional information. With their constant repeating of "why," they may have discovered instant replay long before it became popularized by television.

In addition to asking why, children also ask how. I can still remember asking one of my grandmothers how to hold a needle. As a small child I was fascinated whenever I saw my grandmother do any hand sewing. She was so skillful with a needle that I was captivated each time I watched her make the needle fly through the fabric. After spending several days trying to learn by myself, I finally asked, "HOW do you do that?" What I had done was typical of what many children and adults do. Wanting to learn something, I initially struggled to learn by myself. Then after discovering I needed help, I went to an expert. By asking my grandmother how, I had invited her to share some of her knowledge and expertise. At a later time I found that information useful when reading a book on sewing.

Rather than wait for children to ask us how to do something, we frequently tell them what we know. Typically we do that when wanting them to learn something in particular, such as how to take care of their toys, mow the grass, set the table, follow a recipe, protect themselves from strangers, use the telephone for an emergency, or be careful when crossing a street.

We share knowledge also through unexpected and unplanned experiences. A neighbor experienced such a moment the day she observed her daughter putting water in a plugged-in steam iron. She asked her daughter if she had ever read the directions that came with the iron: "Be sure to unplug iron before adding water to it." Debbie assured her mother that she had but that she never paid much attention to them because she didn't think putting water in the old iron could hurt it too much. Marge then told her daughter that the purpose of the directions was not for the protection of the iron but instead was for user safety. Putting water into a plugged-in iron could cause an electrical shock. Debbie experienced the reality of the manufacturer's written words of caution through the words of wisdom her mother shared.

Overhearing others talk is another way children learn. Most of us, I imagine, have memories to share about things we learned when we listened in on adult conversations. One mother, Kathryn, told me that she fondly recalls listening to the adult talk at family gatherings when she was a child. Kathryn said that after everyone had stuffed themselves with food, the men moved to the living room, porch, or yard and discussed the latest farm news—weather, machinery, planting, harvesting, and prices. The women, meanwhile, moved to the kitchen and discussed the latest family news—birthdays, weddings, engagements, and their children's school work and other activities. Even though Kathryn was usually not a part of the conversations, she was learning from the conversations. She was learning that some of the purposes for talking included sharing information, discussing issues, and on occasion debating or disagreeing. Additionally, Kathryn, who lived in the city, was learning something about farm life. That knowledge then came in handy when she was reading anything that was related to farming, allowing her to visualize more easily farm concepts that otherwise might have been difficult for her to conceptualize.

In each instance of talking with and listening to others talk, children learn both about the world that surrounds them and how language functions. That knowledge is then available to them when reading and writing.

6 Children and parents as learning partners

The learning partnership includes working with and observing others

Several years ago a friend told me how much her children learned when working with her in the kitchen. Marcella said that when her children were young, one of the things they enjoyed was helping her do the dishes. Even though they were often in her way, they learned how to measure the detergent, regulate the water temperature, and rinse and wipe the dishes. In addition to learning something about detergents, water temperature, and rinsing and drying, my friend told me that her children were also learning to assume a family responsibility. After Marcella finished talking, I reminded her that they were also extending their vocabulary, learning to follow directions, and learning to participate in a conversation.

After hearing me tell the above story, another mother related a similar story. Clare said that whenever she was busy cooking, Pamela, her daughter, wanted to be right at her elbow. For safety's sake, Clare put Pam in her high chair, gave her some cooking utensils to play with, and then placed the chair close enough so that Pam could see what her mother was doing. Even when she was cooking at the stove, Clare did this. When Clare's mother first saw her granddaughter sitting near the stove, she was horrified until Clare assured her that Pam was safe there because she was far enough away from the stove but could still see all that was going on.

While trying to observe their parents in the kitchen, Pam and other children work on learning about food preparation. As a result of their observations and their own explorations, they learn about whipping, stirring, blending, baking, chilling, or freezing foods; about adding salt to bring out the flavor of some foods and adding sugar to counteract the acidity in other foods; or about adding lemon juice to prevent some foods from turning brown. They also learn about such things as making pretty designs and writing messages on birthday or special anniversary cakes as well as their cultural, ethnic,

Working with and observing others 7

and religious background when helping to prepare foods for special family dinners. Thus, while at their parents' elbows, children are in a position to learn that cooking includes knowledge of science, math, art, and language.

Children demonstrate what they are learning when they try out cooking for themselves. Their first attempts are usually to mix dirt and water together to make mud pies. After thoroughly mixing the dirt and water and forming the pies, they put them in a safe place to dry. To show they are learning something about manners as well, children often like to share their pies with us or another individual who is willing to play their game.

Although children learn extensively when helping or observing their parents prepare meals, the learning is not limited to the kitchen. They also learn when helping with the family laundry, cleaning the house, pumping up a flat tire, and planting the garden. Through any of these activities, children learn not only how to do the activity but also something about measurement, pressure, chemicals, and electricity.

By doing these kinds of things, children extend their knowledge of the world, including their knowledge of language. As mentioned earlier, children become walking dictionaries due in no small part to the talking they hear and the talking they themselves do while engaged in family chores. Among other things they learn the names of products, as illustrated by a four-year-old who requested Dijon mustard for her sandwich. Because they hear others using them in different situations, they also learn that certain words have more than one meaning, such as *catchup*, which in one situation means what is poured on a hamburger and in another situation means to hurry and catch up with someone. The knowledge children have of words and the way they are used is helpful when they encounter them in books or want to use them in writing.

Because reading and writing are entailed in many of these activities, children are in a perfect environment to learn that reading sources extend beyond books, news-

8 Children and parents as learning partners

papers, and magazines to such things as a recipe or a set of directions on the bleach bottle and that writing can be a shopping list or a note left for the trash collector.

The learning partnership includes play and family recreation

Although television may occupy much of our indoor leisure time, a number of us still enjoy playing cards and board games with children. Among the favorite games that many of us enjoy are those we played when we were kids. In particular, they include Fish, Hearts, War, Old Maid, Monopoly, Clue, Tripoly, checkers, chess, and jigsaw puzzles. Of recent date Trivial Pursuit, Pictionary, and video games have become popular family activities.

One of the nice features about most of these games is that they are ageless and can be enjoyed in a multiage group. Perhaps the rules may need to be adjusted a bit for the younger players, but they soon catch on and the rule adjustment is no longer needed. Whenever I'm playing games with my young neighbor friends, I enjoy observing the two older children, a seven-year-old and a five-year-old, help their three-year-old brother participate. If the game is one I'm either not familiar with or haven't played for quite some time, the two older children help me to participate, too. In this situation they are the teachers and I am the learner.

When playing with or watching others play board games, children learn to follow directions, to play fair, and to have acceptable behavior. They also learn to add, to compare numbers, to ask questions, and to form strategies. Although not intended to do so, many board games also foster literacy. Initially players need to read the directions in order to know how to play the game. Later, rereading the directions may be necessary to clarify the rules of the game. At times rereading the directions is not sufficient. Not too long ago a father told me that he and his family had a lively discussion on whether or not a particular play was within the rules of a game they were playing. To resolve the argument he and one

Play and family recreation 9

of his daughters wrote to the company and asked for clarification. In this instance the father was not only helping his daughter learn to play a game but also helping her learn that adults, too, sometimes have difficulty interpreting written rules.

Another form of indoor play and recreation that many families enjoy is music. We entertain ourselves by playing instruments, records, tapes, or the radio and often sing, hum, or whistle as we go about our work and play. Even those of us who can't carry a tune enjoy humming or making up little songs when rocking an infant at bedtime. Children who take music lessons are often prevailed upon to entertain by performing what they are learning. Children who have no musical instrument to play often devise their own instruments, using table tops for drums, pan lids for cymbals, or balloons for wind instruments. At times children enlist others to help them make instruments. No doubt most of us have been the expert they turn to when they need help making a drum by stretching a piece of cloth over the open end of an empty coffee can or box.

Each instance of children singing or playing a real or make-believe instrument helps them tune into the sound and feel of music. They explore rhythm and develop a sense for the beat, or pulse, of music. They also develop a sense for pitch and tone as well as words when they sing along with others. All of these experiences help children tune into the sounds, including language, that surround them.

Although storytelling as a form of family recreation may not be as prevalent as in days gone by, many people share parts of their childhood by telling stories about it. The "when I was your age" story is a favorite device many parents use to convince a son or daughter to do something, such as walk or ride their bicycle instead of expecting someone to chauffeur them.

Because of the recent interest in finding one's roots, some families record stories that older family members have to tell about themselves. These memories often take the form of a story and help children learn not only

10 Children and parents as learning partners

about storytelling but also about their heritage. Thus a sense of family history is captured while at the same time the art of storytelling is revitalized.

One of the nice features of storytelling is that it provides children with a rich source of information. This information, then, is available to children when they read stories or write their own.

For many of us, television is also a form of family entertainment. We watch movies and sporting events that might be too costly to see otherwise, and we enjoy programs such as sitcoms, miniseries, and documentaries that introduce us to a world outside of our living rooms. The programs, in addition to providing entertainment, help us learn about languages and dialects other than our own, about places we may never visit, and about people we may never meet. Commercials and public service announcements, too, can be informative. They tell us about such things as the need for more fiber and less sugar in our diets, the value in regular dental checkups and teeth care, and the reasons why we should avoid drugs, tobacco, and strangers.

When monitoring television programs with children, we help them learn to be discriminating in program selection, to be aware of the pros and cons of various issues, to question information presented on programs and in commercials, and to detect biases and prejudices. By discussing the programs with them, we help children extend their learning. They in turn help us learn what they are thinking, how they react to various issues, and what interests them. When we write to the networks to let them know our feelings about programs we find inappropriate for children, we demonstrate having a social conscience.

Other forms of entertainment and recreation many families enjoy are outdoor games. Because baseball—or softball—requires little equipment, can be played in most yards or open lots, and is enjoyed by people of all ages, it is one of the most popular outdoor games. The first of many ball games begins when someone tosses a ball back and forth to a toddler. Then as children are capable, they are given advice on how to hold a bat and

Play and family recreation **11**

swing it. Eventually they are invited to join in playing a ball game along with other family members. At times the rules may need to be adjusted to accommodate new members of the team: for example, allowing them to have more attempts to hit the ball, to have help in holding the bat, and to run a shorter base line. Adjustments in the rules often occur when a younger child is needed in order for the game to go on. As the child gets older, or more adept, the rules are adapted to be closer to family, neighborhood, or game standards. At the same time, even the very young child is not permitted to revamp the rules to suit himself or herself without regard for the other players. An early lesson is learned when children realize that the breaking of one rule is not treated the same as the breaking of another rule. Thus, in backyards, driveways, and neighborhood parks children and parents learn from each other something about both sports and sportsmanship.

Other outdoor activities that many families enjoy include picnicking, fishing, swimming, sledding, or hiking as well as tending a garden, repairing old cars, and flying kites. When involved in any of these or other family activities, children learn about the activity itself as well as often develop a lifelong recreational interest. At times the interest may not be in actually participating in the activity but in reading about it.

When children have no one to play with, they usually initiate their own play. Much of the play that they initiate reflects the work they see others perform. They pretend to be moms and dads, carpenters, doctors, mechanics, teachers, farmers, truck drivers, chemists, astronauts, or ball players. With each engagement in a play activity, children work at learning what they want to know. As Carolyn Burke, a researcher and teacher-educator, has suggested, play is a low-stress way of learning (personal communication, 1987). In the low-stress situation children experiment, explore, and test out what they can learn about such things as hammering a nail, bandaging a doll's arm, shoveling sand, flying a kite, playing ball, or keeping score.

Many of us encourage children's play experiences by

12 Children and parents as learning partners

providing them with toys that resemble adult tools and equipment. We buy dolls, trucks, wagons, train sets, medicine kits, sports equipment, sand pails, shovels, and any number of other toys that help children learn. Among the many things children learn when playing with toys—both those we provide as well as those they devise for themselves—is to be in command. If in doubt about play helping children learn to be in command, all we need to do is watch how they coach and referee their own games. They need no adult to help them choose up sides, to establish rules of play, to improvise equipment, or to settle arguments. Occasionally children will write their own list of rules. Then when disagreements arise, they refer to the rules they've imposed on themselves. Most often, though, the winning or losing of the game itself is immaterial. It is the process of playing that is important, and with each new game the process is repeated.

Just as playing with toys and games is an important part in overall learning, playing with language is an important part in language learning. The language play, as already mentioned, begins when infants spend great lengths of time smacking their lips together and blowing through them. Gradually all of the playing around pays off when a child makes sounds that resemble "mama," "baba," "dada," or "papa"—incidentally, sounds that most of us excitedly identify as our baby's first utterance of "mommy," "baby," "daddy," or "papa."

When children are older they continue to play with language. They talk to themselves and pretend they are any number of different people or characters from real life or from books. They chant jump-rope rhymes, make up riddles or jokes, and use puns. Martin, an eight-year-old, can help us appreciate the fact that he enjoys playing with language when he coins a new word. Martin and his friends Derek, Andrew, and Bill were talking about a play script they were writing when they decided Derek would be the main character, King Hyena. After the boys made that decision, Martin grinned and said, "I guess we'll have to call Derek "Your Royal Hyenaness.' " The knowledge Martin has gained from playing with new

An invitation to explore and reflect **13**

words will help him when he meets other authors who coin words.

Many children play with language by reading a favorite story or book to themselves or to an imaginary friend. They change their voices to suit the characters in the story and at times embellish or slightly change the story by adding something from their own experiences. For example, four-year-old Don used his name instead of the name *Milton* when reading *Milton The Early Riser*, a story written by Robert Kraus. Each time the name *Milton* appeared in the story, Don personalized it by substituting his own name. What Don did is significant because it indicates he understands the story.

Children also enjoy playing with language by writing. They write their own shopping lists as well as notes and letters to others. And even though adults may be unable to read or figure out what the child has written, the important thing is that the child is experimenting, exploring, and testing what writers do when they write. (In chapter 4, I'll talk more about this concept.)

An invitation to explore and reflect

As a means of exploring the learning partnership you and your children have established, I invite you to take a close look at the many things you do throughout the day that enhance and extend your children's learning, including reading and writing. To do that, I suggest you select a family activity, such as doing dishes, raking leaves, polishing the car, hoeing in the garden, going to the shopping mall, or reading a letter from grandparents. Then make a mental note of the knowledge and information you share with your children, the directions you give them, the questions they ask, and the responses you give. I think you will realize that you and your children have established a rich learning partnership.

As a means of reflecting upon what you learn, you may want to record what you discovered in a scrapbook. If you have not started to keep one, now is the time to begin. Having an anecdotal record will provide you with a lasting memory of the special sayings your children

14 Children and parents as learning partners

express as well as with tangible evidence of the role you play in your children's oral and written language growth. The recording need not be extensive. Your children's ages, the date, and a few words will do.

You might find it insightful to share your scrapbook with others. But when you share what you are learning with your family and friends, keep in mind that you provide your children with unique learning opportunities. Your experiences, therefore, will not be the same as those other families have. Because no two families are the same, the partnerships will differ.

In chapter 2 I will continue to discuss the child-parent partnership by focusing on the environmental language, or print, that surrounds our children and how we use that print. I will look, in particular, at the reading and writing we do that invites children into the world of literacy.

ENVIRONMENTAL LANGUAGE IS EVERYWHERE

Children live in a print-saturated environment and from a remarkably early age attempt to make sense of the print that surrounds them.

Martha, a four-year-old, can help us realize that environmental language is everywhere, even in litter. When Martha and her family were taking a long trip by car that included driving through the Rocky Mountains, they stopped to enjoy the scenery. Unfortunately, the natural beauty was not quite as unspoiled up close as it had seemed from a distance, as Martha's father pointed out when he discovered evidence that some litterbugs had visited the area. Martha, who had been paying more attention to the litter than to the scenery, agreed with her father: "Look, they were drinking Coke."

Although litter is distasteful, it does seem to be everywhere, and obviously children like Martha are not oblivious to the print on it. Litter is, of course, only one example of the almost overwhelming amount of environmental language in which children are immersed. Children live in a print-saturated environment and from a remarkably early age attempt to make sense of the print that surrounds them. Among the many things they do is ask questions about it, such as "What does *outrageous* mean?" when overhearing a parent comment about the price on a price tag; "How do you pronounce *A l i q u i p p a*?" when seeing a city limits sign; or "How do you spell *guh*?" when wanting to know what letter to use at the end of the word *dog*. Such questioning indicates children are entering the world of reading and writing. They have taken notice of what others do and want to do likewise.

The world of reading that children want to enter

With the many opportunities children have to see others read and talk about print, we should not be surprised that they, too, want to do the same. Martha, the youngster who noticed that some litterbugs had been drinking Coke, demonstrates that she was entering the world of reading when commenting about the litter she saw. Although Martha's parents might have wished that she pay attention to the majestic surroundings, Martha was more intent on looking at the litter and taking note of the print on it. To help Martha and other readers do that, the distributors of Coke have supplied information that

18 Environmental language is everywhere

they hope will make their product easy to identify, including the distinctive shape or color of the container and the registered Coca-Cola Company trademark script. The Coca-Cola Company would certainly be pleased that the print they provided did not go unnoticed by Martha.

To have an idea of the vast amount of print children encounter on a regular basis, we can begin by sorting through the books, newspapers, and magazines many of us read. Then we can rifle through our kitchen cabinets—full of cereal boxes, canned goods, and junk food—peruse our coupon file and recipe box, check the junk mail, watch a bit of advertising on television, and take note of messages on billboards and bumper stickers. While browsing through the print that surrounds us, we can also take note of the various ways we use that print.

When thinking of the different kinds of reading most people do, the first things that usually come to mind are books, newspapers, and magazines. We read books to help us keep up to date on our work, to learn new information, and to provide entertainment. We also read books to and with our children, particularly at bedtime. We read newspapers to help us keep abreast of local, national, and international news; to follow favorite columnists and comic strips; and to check out the ads. Some of us also enjoy reading portions of the newspaper, particularly the comics, with our children. And we read magazines to help us learn more about our hobbies, special interests, and work. We often read magazines such as *National Geographic* with our children as well as magazines written especially for children such as *National Geographic World, Highlights for Children* and *Ebony Jr.*! to name but a few. (A short bibliography of children's magazines can be found at the end of this book.)

The world of reading extends beyond books, newspapers, and magazines, though—a discovery a father made a couple of years ago. When I suggested to a group of parents that they probably read more than books, newspapers, and magazines, one of the fathers, John, contended that he had very little time to do any reading. After I insisted that he probably did more than he re-

The world of reading that children want to enter **19**

alized, John hesitantly asked, "Would clipping coupons be considered reading?" Because he was unemployed, John supplemented his wife's income by clipping coupons. As he explained, "During the day, while I'm home with the baby, I cut out the coupons. Then at night, when the older kids get through with their homework, we sort through the coupons and check for their value, their expiration dates, and directions on where to write to receive any refunds. You'd be surprised how much money we've made. It takes a little work, but it sure helps buy a few groceries."

After John finished talking, several people began to develop a list of other reading sources their children see them use. Initially they listed reading sources found in their kitchen cabinets—canned goods, cereal boxes, and spices. Then they added recipes, sewing patterns, road maps, tax forms, and directions for assembling tools or toys. Of course, reading directions for unassembled products can be quite frustrating for some of us. Nevertheless, such experiences can be valuable. Children who know that their parents are not always successful as readers will have a better understanding that adults, too, encounter problems when they read.

Sometimes we read for special purposes that pertain to our children. A friend has learned to read all the small print found on food products because her son has a low tolerance level for sugar. Cathy said her son has also learned to check out that same information when they go shopping. Thus, because of a health need, Cathy is helping her son learn to look for certain information found on labels.

Other labels that most of us read are those found on items such as toothpaste tubes, medicine bottles, paint cans, and appliances. In addition to providing the name of the product, manufacturers include other information. They supply ingredients, pictures, recipes, directions, and information about the volume or size and the quality of the product. Although most manufacturers are not engaged in teaching literacy, they call attention to the names of products and their attributes by using bold and/or colored print often accompanied by a pic-

20 Environmental language is everywhere

ture. All of that special packaging invites adults and children to read the product name and something about it. We, too, call attention to that print when we talk about it. Actually, most of us do more talking about print than we realize. For example, when driving, we talk about and point to store logos, street signs, and highway markers. We say such things as "Did that sign say Prospect Avenue?" and "Watch for the sign that says Murphysboro because that's where we have to get off."

Talking about print helps children in many ways. It helps them to focus on vocabulary they might not encounter in their oral language environment, to distinguish the difference between information found on street signs and that found on milk cartons or in directions, and to have an insight into the thinking process we go through whenever commenting about street signs, verifying directions, or asking how to spell words.

I think one of the reasons children recognize the print on their favorite cereal is because they have seen it and heard others talk about it on television. To illustrate that children are not oblivious to the print they see on TV, I like to share the following story a friend told me a number of years ago about her three-year-old son.

While Mary and her husband were watching TV, Tommy was playing nearby and seemingly not paying attention to the program his parents were watching. At commercial time though, Tommy stopped playing with his toys and began to listen to a man talk about Ajax cleanser. When the commercial was over, Tommy ran to the kitchen and returned with a can of the cleanser.

Mary's story can help us realize that print is a part of television, too. The print includes weather warning messages; program introductions; epilogues; lists of characters, credits, and titles; and copyright information. It also includes messages suggesting the need for parental guidance if children watch particular shows and addresses to write for more information about a product or program. In addition to television announcers calling attention to all of this print when they read product names and messages that appear on the screen, viewers, too, call attention to that print when they talk about what

The world of reading that children want to enter **21**

they are viewing. All of this attention to print does not go unnoticed by children, as Tommy demonstrated.

Another way children show they take note of print information found on television, labels, signs, and appliances is by asking questions about it. One of my first memories of asking a question about print was when I was five years old. While visiting an aunt, I became intrigued with the word *Superior* on the oven door and wanted to know what it said. My aunt, instead of telling me what the word was, created a song on the spot: "S u p e r i o r, that says Superior." Eventually I began to sing along with her as we both pointed to the word. To this day, I can still visualize the word *Superior* etched in the grey-and-white oven door.

Other print that is important in our lives is the mail. For many of us, a special moment of the day is the arrival of the daily mail. We look for letters from family members and friends, often sharing the news by reading portions to our children. Less eagerly we open and read the monthly bills, often commenting about how high the bill is and recounting the purchases we've made while checking it for accuracy.

Most of us receive unsolicited mail, which we may read if it has some value or special announcement of interest to us. Otherwise, after a quick glance at the envelope, we usually throw it away. One mother, though, told me she keeps all the junk mail that arrives. Because her younger children complained they never received any mail, Mildred said that she gives them the occupant letters, catalogs, and sale flyers. Now they do not feel left out when others in the family receive mail. They, too, have mail to open. By providing her children with the unsolicited mail, Mildred is inviting them to be a part of the world of literacy along with others in the family.

Recently while talking with a group of parents about reading materials they receive in the mail, one father, Mr. Davis, commented that each spring when the gardening catalogs arrive his son likes to look at them. Mr. Davis also commented that he frequently reads the catalog descriptions of the various fruits, vegetables, trees, and shrubs to his son; includes him in on making out

22 Environmental language is everywhere

the various orders; and lets him help with the gardening. Certainly the companionship that Mr. Davis had established with his five-year-old son was instrumental in helping the little boy discover that gardening catalogs can be enjoyable reading material. Other catalogs children enjoy browsing through are those containing the latest clothing styles, games, toys, and electronic equipment.

The print environment is, of course, not confined to the home. We read outside our homes, too. When shopping, we read logos and signs that help us know where to go to buy shoes, clothing, bicycles, flowers, computers, and any number of other things. When driving, we read signs that help us know where we are, where to turn, where to stop, and when to take precautions. At times we enlist the help of our children in finding a particular place to eat, shop, or stop. When we ask our children to look for a particular sign or landmark, we call their attention to the print. Thus, we should not be surprised that children learn to read certain logos and signs at an early age.

Many of us use the print on signs when playing car games. One popular car game is the alphabet game, where players try to spot each letter of the alphabet. The most exciting part of the game is to see who can be the first person to find a Quaker State motor oil sign when needing a *q* because whoever does also finds *r, s, t,* and *u*. A friend told me that playing the alphabet game helped her to learn that some words have alternative spellings. She said that she still remembers being surprised when seeing a sign advertising barbecue with the word spelled *bar-b-q*.

In recent years many of us have begun to wear print. We wear t-shirts, jackets, and caps that carry greetings, admonishments, advertisements, and pithy sayings stating who we are, where we've been, or what issues we espouse. Athletes may wear on their uniforms club names, logos, numbers, and sometimes the name of the sponsor as well as the player's name. On practically every piece of clothing they make, manufacturers place labels

The world of reading that children want to enter 23

identifying their name and giving directions for washing or cleaning.

We also carry reading material on our cars and trucks in the form of license plates, some of which have messages on them, such as "You've Got a Friend in Pennsylvania." Others of us transport reading materials by attaching bumper stickers that tend to reflect our beliefs about such things as politics, environmental issues, and religion. Several years ago a mother told me that she and her children learned many of the state names and something about them as a result of collecting information from car and truck license plates.

Many reading materials are portable: we can carry reading with us. When traveling, we take along road maps; directions for locating an unfamiliar place; and at times, books, newspapers, magazines, and games. We take something to read while waiting for a bus, train, or plane. As a means of entertaining or keeping youngsters quiet when going to church or special events, we take children's books with us. Because the portability of print is one of its most valuable assets, reading material can always be available. And when we carry reading with us, we establish for both ourselves and our children the lifelong habit of reading for information and for enjoyment.

Children demonstrate they are developing the habit of reading when they carry a book along with them or ask us to help them get a book from the library. Even very young children demonstrate this development when they read a story similar to the way they have heard others read it. Often they take on the pose of an adult reader: sitting in a chair, legs crossed, with favorite book in hand. Even though they may not read the text verbatim, most children tend to read a close facsimile of it and use the same intonation they've heard others use. They look and sound like readers.

The mother of a two-year-old discovered that her son looked and sounded like a reader when he insisted on being the reader at bedtime. One evening when it was time for Robert to go to bed, he insisted

24 Environmental language is everywhere

upon reading his favorite book, *The Carrot Seed* by Ruth Krauss, which is a story about a little boy talking to his father about planting a carrot seed and watching it grow. While listening to Robert read, his mother said that even though he did not read the story as written, she had no problem recognizing who was talking in the story because Robert varied the pitch of his voice much like his father did when reading it. Robert's mother had every right not only to enjoy what he had done but also to rejoice in the fact that he was developing the habit of reading.

Because of the wealth of print that surrounds children, they often encounter it when at home or on a family outing—even to a ball game as Kate, a three-year-old, demonstrated. Kate, her mother, and I had gone to a ball game together, and upon arrival at the ballpark, Kate's mother and I were each given a program. Because Kate was unhappy not to have received one, Kate's mother shared hers. After we were seated, Kate began to look at the program. Suddenly she shouted, "I found my name." Then Kate pointed to the letter *K* in the names Karen and Kevin. Although the names Kate found were not hers, she had found names that began with *K*. And it is significant to note that of all the other print available to her, Kate selected words that were people's names and only those names that began with the letter *K*. *K*, thus, served Kate as her name.

Children encounter literacy each time they see us browse through a newspaper, clip coupons, read directions for assembling toys and tools, check labels on a shopping trip, react to television commercials, or play Trivial Pursuit. And we are involved in their literacy learning each time we ask them to get a can of mushroom soup out of the cupboard, to reach for a can of coffee on the supermarket shelf, to read their favorite story, or to help us figure out the directions for playing a game. Therefore, we should not be surprised that Martha, Tommy, Robert, Kate, and other children have already taken their first step into the world of reading.

The world of writing that children want to enter

At first glance the world of writing may not appear to be as full as the world of reading is. But after exploring the daily writing we do—notes to ourselves, personal and business letters, reminders on the calendar, shopping lists, labels for foods in the freezer, checks, or a message on a birthday cake—most of us are surprised to discover that we do more writing than we think.

Although letter writing may not be as popular as it once was because of the convenience of using the telephone, many of us still write to keep in touch with family and friends and to keep a record of personal and business plans. Some of us include our children when we write letters, especially those to family members, and on occasion some of us include them even when writing business letters. Several years ago a father related that prior to taking a family vacation, he asked his ten-year-old son to help write letters to a number of state tourism departments requesting road and travel information. Ben, the father, said that all of the states responded, with many sending road maps and brochures about geographic points of interest and special events being held that summer.

When Ben and his older son began to receive mail every few days, his five-year-old son wanted to know why he never received any. At that time, Ben realized Jason should have been a part of the project. "In the future," Ben said, "I'll include Jason, too." Because Jason wanted to be a part of the world of writing his older brother and father were in, he invited himself to join them. Fortunately his father accepted his invitation. In doing so, Ben respected his son's desire to want to write and also provided himself with an opportunity to appreciate some of his son's early writing efforts.

After hearing how beneficial Ben's family letter-writing activity had been, a mother mentioned that she and her youngsters had often talked about writing for the tourist information they see advertised on television or in magazines but had never done it. Now she was eager

26 Environmental language is everywhere

to write for some of that information in order to find out about places they might like to visit or know more about.

Sending birthday, anniversary, and other special greeting cards is a way many of us keep in touch with one another. At times we add a personal touch by designing our own greeting cards or search for just the right card and then add our own personal message to it. To personalize the message even more, we often include writing and drawing our children have done.

Often overlooked in the writing we do are the messages and dates we record on a bulletin board or calendar. Because individual schedules vary, having a family message board helps us remember dentist appointments, Little League practice, music lessons, and other family engagements. Recently a mother told me that because she works outside the home, she and her children have a special message board for the purpose of leaving notes for one another. Karen said that it was not unusual to come home and find a note from her son or daughter telling about a special event such as passing an exam, making the team, or spending the night with a friend. These messages are much like receiving a letter from one of her children and vice versa. The message board is a way for them to keep in touch.

After hearing Karen's story, a friend said that gave him an idea. Because his son usually forgets to tell them where he is going to go to play, Roy said he thought having a message board might work in his family. Everyone could leave a note saying where they had gone and when they would be back. "Perhaps that would cut down the amount of time we spend trying to find Steve." As he talked, Roy remarked that in the process of learning to be considerate of others Steve would also be learning to read and write messages.

Another type of writing is making a shopping list. For many of us, making a shopping list is a necessity. Without it, we often buy what we don't need and forget to buy what we do need. A shopping list also helps us remember information about items we wish to purchase such as brand name, size, color, or quantity. At times we enlist

The world of writing that children want to enter 27

the help of our children and ask them to help make the shopping list. By including our children, we help them learn list making is another form of writing. At times even young children initiate writing their own lists as illustrated by Michael. (See page 56.)

A friend told me that he writes when gardening. In order to remember what he has planted and how to care for it, Matt writes the information on a stick and places it in the ground at planting time. Other types of signs and banners that families make are used to advertise garage sales, to identify a house address, or to greet a special person. Some people even write greetings on the food they eat. Whenever I watch my niece decorate a cake, I'm always intrigued at how artistically she can write a name, date, and greeting with icing. Lisa has told me she learned that skill by helping her mother decorate cakes.

Most children seem to be right underfoot when we are trying to get something done. They stand in our way and want to put their fingers into everything. Although we may not always appreciate their presence, our youngsters are in a perfect position to satisfy their curiosity and to learn about their world. Such is the case when children are curious about what writers do. They enjoy testing a pencil, pen, or crayon by making marks on paper similar to those they've seen others make. This exploring and testing is an important aspect of children's writing development. As we shall see in chapter 4, even though we may not be able to decipher what some children write, they will proudly tell us what they have written or drawn.

In order to keep them occupied while we pay bills, write a letter, or make out a grocery list, some of us put young children in a highchair and provide them with their own paper and pencil or crayons. Some of us even provide a special writing spot for them when we want to keep them out of our way or the way of others in the family. A friend of mine said she solved the problem of her two little girls pestering their older brothers and sisters during homework time. By putting a table leaf across the arms of a large chair, Mary made a desk for

28 Environmental language is everywhere

the preschoolers. Then the girls could do their "homework" too and share it with others nearby. At the same time, their mother established that she valued both the younger children's desire to write while others were writing and the older children's right to get their homework done.

Writing letters, sending special greetings cards, setting up message boards, making shopping lists, even labeling the garden plants and decorating cakes are all examples of what we do to introduce our children to the world of writing. Children who are encouraged to participate in this writing are well on their way to becoming capable writers long before they begin formal schooling.

An invitation to explore and reflect

As a means of exploring and reflecting upon the environmental language in your children's world, I invite you to take a trip around your home and notice the variety of reading and writing you do there. To begin your trip, first make a mental note of all the print you use. Check out the print in your home—the kitchen, living room, family room, bedrooms, bathroom, garage, and basement—and outside of your home—street signs, store logos, banners, and billboards. I think you will find your environment is saturated with print, probably more print than you ever use. But it is there in the event you want to use it for either reading or writing.

Next, explore the ways you and your children use the print. To do that, select a family activity in which you can easily include your children, such as grocery shopping. Then notice the print you and your children read before going to the store. Observe any comments or questions your children have about the print and the responses you make. While writing your shopping list, ask your children to write one for themselves. Watch what they do when writing, and listen to anything they have to say about it. (You may want to refer to chapter 4 to get some idea of what to look for in your children's writing.) Watch what they do while you are writing and listen for any comments they make.

An invitation to explore and reflect **29**

On the way to the store, notice any talking you do about the signs and logos along the way. Take note of what you say and how your children respond. Listen to any comments they make. In general, tune into what you both say about the print and how you respond to one another.

While shopping, ask your children to help you find some of the items. Notice what information they use. Be sure to notice what your children do with their own shopping list.

When you get home, ask your children to help you put the groceries away. Again observe the comments they make, and be on the lookout for remarks about products you purchased as well as remarks about other print they saw in the store, in the shopping mall, or on the billboards and highway signs.

Then take time to reflect upon the print environment itself and what you and your children did to use the print. You may want to write about your experience as well. If you have already begun a scrapbook, just add a few words that will remind you of this experience. Then as you have other experiences, you can add them to your scrapbook. If you have access to a camera, you can include a picture of your children reading a label or writing the shopping list. Keeping the shopping list is a good idea, too. By doing this, you will have a permanent record of your children's growth in reading and writing.

Because reading books with children is a special kind of reading moment, I will talk about it in chapter 3.

3

READING BOOKS WITH CHILDREN

Each time we read a book with a child is a special learning moment.

When parents talk with one another, one of the things they enjoy doing is telling stories about their children. Martha's father did this when he told about Martha discovering literacy in litter. A story I like to share took place several years ago, also on a family driving trip. Because I knew spending a number of days riding in the car would be a trying time for my three-year-old son, I packed several puzzles and toys that I thought would keep him entertained and out of mischief. When David grew tired of those playthings, I bought a couple of books to read to him. Although not familiar with either of the books, I chose them because they had interesting pictures. Little did I realize one of the books, *The Owl and the Pussy Cat*, a nonsense verse by Edward Lear, would be an excellent choice.

After looking through the book and talking about the pictures with David, I began to read it to him. When I finished, he wanted me to read it to him again and again. For the next couple of days that was the only book he wanted to listen to. Finally in exasperation I said, "If you want to hear that story again, you're going to have to read it to yourself." In a few minutes, David began to do just that. As he read the first part, my husband and I couldn't believe what we were hearing:

> *The Owl and the Pussy-Cat went to sea*
> *In a beautiful pea-green boat,*
>
> *They took some honey, and plenty of money,*
> *Wrapped up in a five-pound note.*

Much to our amazement, David held the book, turned the pages in the appropriate spots, and read with much the same intonation he had heard me use. Of course our reactions were those of typical proud parents. We could hardly wait to tell everyone what he had done.

Since that time, I've learned that what David did was not unusual. He was doing what many other children who have repeatedly heard their favorite stories do. He was picking up on the interesting rhythmical and rhyming patterns of *The Owl and the Pussy Cat*. Although I rather doubt he grasped what pea-green boats, plenty of money, and five-pound notes were, David was taking

32 Reading books with children

one of his first steps into the world of reading. I've also learned that unknowingly we had discovered what Huey in 1908 suggested: "The secret of it all lies in the parents reading aloud to and with the child" (p. 332). While reading with our son, we were introducing him to the world of books. We were helping him learn that books have new and interesting words in them as well as organizational patterns and that they are filled with information.

When we read a book with our children, it is oftentimes an unplanned moment. The moment just seems to occur whenever we pick up a book and read to entertain, distract, or comfort our youngsters. We do this when taking our children to see the doctor or dentist, when attempting to quiet them in church, and when consoling them after a fall or other unpleasant experience. In this way, we build many pleasant memories.

At other times, the shared reading moments are planned. Recently a father told me he can still remember that when he was a child, Sunday afternoon was a special time for his father to read to him. Joe said that each Sunday he would crawl up on his father's lap and wait for him to read aloud the "funnies." Joe now reads the comics to his own children and continues to talk with his dad about favorites they both enjoy reading.

Because he has fond memories of his father reading the comics to him, Joe is carrying on a family tradition. Other reading traditions that many families continue from one generation to the next include reading scriptures, seasonal books such as *A Christmas Carol*, and bedtime stories.

For many of us, the story at bedtime is a time to cuddle up next to our youngsters, to enjoy a moment of peace and relaxation, to build values through discussion, and to store up some good memories. According to a friend of mine, one of her fondest childhood memories was cuddling up with either her parents or grandparents and listening to a bedtime story. "Without a doubt," Heather said, "the feeling I had while listening to my parents and grandparents read to me colored my feelings toward books." A special book that remains in my memory is *Hans Brinker or The Silver Skates* by Mabel Mapes Dodge. Although the book was interesting and opened new doors for me, one of the major reasons that it is memorable is due to the circumstances in which my mother shared the book with my brother and me. In my mind's eye, I can still remember her telling us each evening that she would read the next chapter as soon as we finished our homework. Then while she stretched out on the couch, my brother and I hovered nearby. Periodically we would stop to question her about something. At other times, when she thought we might not understand a particular part of the story, she would stop and explain it to us. Because of the feelings generated by that warm and supportive learning environment, that book remains one of my favorites.

Why read books to children?

Through these experiences, we can learn that one of the benefits of reading books to children is that it provides them with a sense of security and peace and us with an opportunity to share a special moment with them. But the benefits are not limited to that. Reading to children helps them open up their world, learn concepts without having to worry about words, preview books, bridge the gap between oral language and written language, and overcome any fear of words they may have.

No doubt most of us can recall a time when our world was opened up because someone read to us. As mentioned earlier, I often recall the winter when my mother read *Hans Brinker or the Silver Skates* to my brother and me. While my mother read about Hans and his family, I tried to imagine what living in a country with canals and windmills would be like. Because I wanted to learn more about that far-away country, each time I went to the library I tried to find other books about Holland. My mother's reading

34 Reading books with children

not only opened up my world, it also encouraged me to explore on my own.

Books that stimulate a child's interest soon become favorites, and most children never cease listening to someone read them over and over again. A friend told me that before his son Mark went to school he knew many things about how dinosaurs lived and reasons why people think they became extinct. Mark had learned these things as a result of his parents reading books about dinosaurs to him. Even though Mark's parents may have grown tired of reading about them, each time they did, Mark could concentrate on learning about dinosaurs without having to struggle with the words. Thus, reading to children helps them focus on ideas and concepts.

Rereading children's favorite books is beneficial, too. Each time children listen to repeated readings of a book, they can "flush out" new information. When they flush out each bit of new information, children can mesh that information with what they already know. Rereading the same material to children, therefore, helps them affirm previously held information while at the same time helps them extend the knowledge they already have.

Children who have repeatedly heard their favorite books will often read them to themselves or to any other willing individual. Although they may not read the book verbatim, children usually approximate it rather closely. On occasion children may embellish it by adding something from their own experience. Yet when children embellish, they rarely change the author's overall meaning.

Another important reason to read, as well as reread, to children is that it can act as a preview for a book they may want to read for themselves at a later time. As children listen, they can focus on the meaning of the story and get a general idea about it. Having a general sense about the story helps children when they want to read the story independently. Books that may be somewhat difficult for children to enjoy reading by themselves are particularly good read-aloud books. Later on, when

Why read books to children? **35**

youngsters want to read those books independently, they've already had a preview.

Although many of the books children enjoy listening to include fairy tales, legends, myths, and adventures of people and animals in far away lands, they also enjoy books of nursery rhymes, nonsense verse, and riddles. Even though children may not know what many of the Mother Goose nursery rhymes mean, they like the musical quality of such rhymes as "Hickory Dickory Dock," "Hey, Diddle Diddle," and "To Market, To Market." These and other rhymes invite children to read, sing along, and join in any play activities that may accompany them. Because many of these stories and rhymes are a part of our oral tradition, reading them to children helps them bridge the gap between oral language and written language.

When children get older, sometimes they are afraid to read because they don't know all the words; therefore, reading to them is a particularly good idea. Stephanie, a seven-year-old neighbor, was just such a child. Because Stephanie was receiving low grades in reading, her mother asked if I would work with her. One of the things I soon discovered about Stephanie was that she had a fear of not knowing all the words. Each time I asked her to read anything, big tears welled up in her eyes. Therefore, rather than insist that Stephanie read to me, I read to her instead. For several weeks I read stories that I thought would invite Stephanie to chime in and begin to read with me. Gradually, she became less fearful of the words and began to read parts of the story with me. Eventually, when Stephanie felt comfortable with a book, she wanted to read it herself.

As can be seen, reading with children helps them learn about people and animals of other lands; about make-believe giants, ogres, and fairies; or about space, mountains, and deserts. Because books often include characters who talk and say such things as "I could not" rather than "I couldn't" and use unfamiliar colloquialisms, such as "to *fetch* a pail of water," reading to children also helps

36 Reading books with children

them learn that the language of books often differs from the language they hear in other parts of their daily lives. And, it helps them to undertake reading for themselves.

What makes a book hold a child's interest?

Earlier I mentioned that *The Owl and the Pussy Cat* had been highly successful in holding my son's interest. One of the reasons for that was due to the fact we previewed it first by talking about the pictures. Having some idea about the characters and what they did then helped him to follow along. Thus previewing a book by looking at the pictures or other visual aids, relating it to other familiar stories, and discussing unfamiliar concepts all help to make a book hold a child's interest.

Another thing that helps to make a book hold a child's interest is the way the story is constructed. Once I had given *Seven Little Rabbits* by John Becker to a two-year-old. Several days later I stopped by to visit his mother. When I arrived, Kevin was fussy and his mother was momentarily occupied. To help pacify him, I began to read *Seven Little Rabbits*. After a few minutes Kevin's mother came into the living room and asked, "Where's Kevin?" As I pointed to her son snuggled up beside me in the chair, she said, "He's never that quiet. What did you do, mesmerize him?" In a way Kevin was mesmerized, not by me but by the story that begins:

> *Seven little rabbits*
> *Walkin' down the road*
> *Walkin' down the road*
> *Seven little rabbits*
> *Walkin' down the road*
> *To call on old friend toad.*
>
> *One little rabbit*
> *Said he was tired*
> *Walkin' down the road*
> *Walkin' down the road*

What makes a book hold a child's interest? **37**

> *One little rabbit*
> *Said he was tired*
> *Walkin' down the road*
> *To call on old friend toad.*
>
> *So*
> *Seven little rabbits*
> *Turned around*
> *Until they found*
> *Down in the ground*
> *A hole*
> *Built by a mole.*
>
> *Seven little rabbits*
> *Went down the hole*
> *Built by the mole*
> *Down in the ground*
> *Until they found*
> *A den.*
>
> *Then*
> *The seventh little rabbit*
> *Went to sleep—*
> *Shh, don't say "Peep"—*
> *He's tucked in bed*
> *And now, instead, there are . . .*

To help Kevin's mother understand why he retained interest in the book, we discussed the repetition, which helps create a sense of rhythm; the familiar sequence of counting, in reverse order, which helps the listener anticipate what happens next; and the illustrations, which help children follow the story—the rabbits go to sleep one by one, have human characteristics, and do things children themselves might do, such as pick flowers, go on a picnic, take pictures, and go wading. Because of the predictable structure of the book, Kevin found it easy to follow and eventually began to chime in with whomever read it to him. As he grows older, Kevin's knowledge of the predictability of texts will enable him to become a more proficient reader.

According to Lynn Rhodes (1981), a mother and

38 Reading books with children

teacher educator, books having repetitive or cumulative patterns; familiar sequences, story lines, or concepts; and/or a close match between illustrations and text help children anticipate and predict what will happen next in the story. The author of *Seven Little Rabbits*, for example, makes effective use of repetition and rhythm, a familiar sequence, and pictures in a way that encourages children to predict what will happen next. Typically, once children figure out the pattern, they begin to chime in with the reader. *It Didn't Frighten Me!* by Goss and Harste is another book that captivates listeners for the same reasons:

> *One pitch black, very dark night,*
> *right after Mom turned off the light,*
> *I looked out my window only to see,*
> *an orange alligator up in my tree!*
>
> *But ... that orange alligator didn't frighten me!*
>
> *One pitch black, very dark night,*
> *right after Mom turned off the light,*
> *I looked out my window only to see,*
> *a purple witch up in my tree!*
>
> *But ... that purple witch didn't frighten me!*

The pattern established on the first page continues as other creatures are introduced.

After hearing the first few pages of *It Didn't Frighten Me*, children begin to expect what will happen next, and even the most reluctant reader enjoys chiming in with the last part, "... that [name of creature] didn't frighten me." In fact, many children are so involved in predicting the text that they easily substitute *scare* for *frighten* without losing the rhythm of the story. This kind of substitution illustrates that the child is focusing on meaning rather than on vocabulary. The recognition that meaning is the primary goal of reading is another characteristic of proficient readers.

Stories that have a cumulative or add-on structure, such as *The Farmer in the Dell*, also invite children to chime

What makes a book hold a child's interest? 39

in. Although perhaps not as popular a game as it once was, on some playgrounds children chant the story, selecting the farmer who selects a wife, who selects a child, and so on. Another similar add-on story is *The Great Big Enormous Turnip* by Alexei Tolstoy. In that story an old man tries to pull up a turnip. When he is unable to do that, an old woman, a granddaughter, a black dog, a cat, and a mouse are added, one by one, to help him. The cumulative pattern in each of these stories invites children to join in because the next event in the story is easy to predict.

Books with familiar sequences are also effective in inviting children to join in. For example, in *The Very Hungry Caterpillar* Eric Carle uses counting and the days of the week, both familiar sequences to children, to tell the story of a caterpillar that eats several foods throughout the week. Beginning on Monday the caterpillar eats one apple; on Tuesday two pears; and so on, until Saturday. Then he eats a variety of foods that result in his having a stomachache. Finally on Sunday, after eating one leaf, the caterpillar feels better, builds a small house, and stays inside until he pushes his way out and becomes a butterfly. Children enjoy predicting which day and number come next. An added feature of the book, which children like, are the holes they can put their fingers into: one hole in the apple, two holes in the pears, and so on.

Another feature of books that hold children's interest is the close match between the illustrations and storyline. (The pictures in *Seven Little Rabbits* played an important part in helping Kevin sustain interest in the story because he could easily follow along by looking at them.) When someone reads the story to children or when they want to read it themselves, the pictures act as a support system. Understanding the value of illustrations and other visual aids, such as maps and diagrams, available in a text can also contribute to a child's development as a successful reader.

Other books children will listen to, even though they may not have some of the above characteristics, are those with familiar concepts in them and those written by the same author. Mark, the little fellow who liked dinosaurs,

40 Reading books with children

is an example of a youngster who found dinosaur books to be interesting although they might not be for another child. Because he had learned so much from listening to his parents read dinosaur books, they held his interest, and he eventually began to read along with either his mother or father.

Because many authors do not dramatically change their style and main characters from one book to the next, reading one book in a series makes others more predictable; the reader knows basically what to expect. To illustrate that point, let me tell you about Beth, who had a common problem. Beth called me one evening to express a concern she had about Ian, her ten-year-old son, who was a reluctant reader. She said Ian read under duress and seldom checked a book out of the library; when he did, he wouldn't read it. Her efforts to get him to read usually ended with mother and son getting angry at one another.

Knowing Ian liked horses, I suggested that Beth try reading *The Black Stallion*, one of Walter Farley's books, to him. Although Farley's book are not new, they still remain popular with many children. Several weeks later Beth called again to say that the book had been a winner because Ian now wanted her to read another of Farley's books. She also commented that coincidentally, Ian had seen the movie version of *The Black Stallion* at school. Now he was eager to read the book himself.

Most librarians report that children who have seen television and movie films that have been adapted from a book then want to read the book. Therefore they're not surprised that many children request books such as *How the Grinch Stole Christmas; A Christmas Carol; Old Yeller*; and *The Lion, the Witch, and the Wardrobe* soon after viewing the film version. Books that are adapted from a film or a television show (books that come *after* the media event) are also favorites of children. In recent years such books include those from *ET, Star Wars*, and *Sesame Street*. In each of these instances, the film or show has acted as a preview for the book.

In addition to the above kinds of books, another kind of book that holds a child's interest is the wordless picture

What makes a book hold a child's interest? **41**

book. (Some libraries list these books as storybooks without words.) In recent years a number of authors have captured the essence of the adage "one picture is worth a thousand words" by telling their stories in what is known as wordless picture books. Below is a sampling of some of the books available. (For a few additional ones, see the list at the end of this book.)

Children familiar with *Goldilocks and the Three Bears* will enjoy *Deep in the Forest* by Brinton Turkle. In this book, a little bear does all the things Goldilocks does when she breaks into the three bears' home. Even those children who have not heard Goldilocks will enjoy listening to someone read the picture story to them.

Another wordless picture book adapted from literature is *Apples* by Nonny Hogrogian. In *Apples*, instead of Johnny Appleseed dropping apple seeds wherever he traveled, a boy, a girl, and a series of animals drop apple cores in an open field that eventually becomes an orchard.

Mitsumasa Anno shares his travels throughout the world in a series of wordless picture books that include *Anno's Journey, Anno's Britain*, and *Anno's U.S.A.* In each of his books Anno hides all the characters he uses to illustrate a particular country amid trees, buildings, and fields. In *Anno's U.S.A.*, for instance, observant picture readers will find Whistler's Mother, individuals who signed the Constitution, and people marching in Macy's parade to name but a few.

A unique feature of John S. Goodall's books is the use of half pages. Readers enjoy looking at one page, then turning a half page to continue the story. Although many books by Goodall are about Paddy, a pig that has many adventures, he has also published others, including *The Story of an English Village*, which illustrates the many changes that occur in a village between the fourteenth and twentieth centuries. Like many wordless picture books, this one is for all ages.

In our endeavors to invite children to read along with us, we need to be mindful that we not overdo it. At times, children only want to listen to someone read to them and not be involved in chiming in. In these instances,

42 Reading books with children

children respond much as they would to a concert, play, or movie. They want to enjoy the performance without talking to anyone. Afterwards, they may want to discuss what they liked or didn't like. At other times, they may prefer to savor the moment quietly. They want no questions or further discussion about the story, only time to relish a memorable moment.

Why listen to children read?

Typically when we think of reading with children, we think of adults reading to children rather than vice versa. But we should not overlook asking children to read to us. When we listen to them read, we gain some insight into what they are learning. Among the things we can discover are the kinds of books they like to read and share, the information they learn from books, and the eagerness—or lack of—they show toward reading.

Although most young children readily want to read to others, some youngsters, particularly when they get a little older, may be hesitant to do so. To help them overcome their reluctance we can do a number of things. We can encourage them to read a book they are already familiar with, to stop and share while they are reading, and to talk about the book after they are finished reading it. We can also respect our chlidren's endeavors to read.

Books we have read and reread to children make good books for them to read to us. Even though everyone is more than familiar with the book, that familiarity is a plus for young readers. It helps make the book predictable. It also helps make the reading less of a chore because they do not have to labor over the words. Not only does reading a familiar book help lessen children's laboring over words, it also helps them hear anew each time they read the book. With each rereading, children can gather new information and confirm what they already know.

Of course, suggesting that a child read a highly predictable books is always a good idea. Any books that have repetitive and cumulative patterns and a close match between illustrations and text are particularly good

Why listen to children read? 43

choices. Once children begin to read the first portion of the story, they usually can predict what will happen in succeeding parts. At times it may be useful for us to read the first section or two, particularly if the youngster is not already familiar with the book. At other times we may want to take turns reading different parts of the book. Because the reading is being shared, the youngster can listen to the development of the story and for new concepts without being responsible for the entire text.

Reading books that have repetitive patterns in them are especially good choices for taking turns. For example, in *It Didn't Frighten Me*, there are a couple of excellent possibilities for each reader to take a turn. One is for each individual to read alternate pages. Another is for one reader to be responsible for the first part of each page and the other reader to be responsible for the second part. When youngsters aren't already familiar with the story, getting it started is advisable. To do that, we can read the first few pages, then ask the youngster if he or she would like to read the next part. Sometimes there is no need for us to offer children an invitation; they just want to chime in.

Plays and books with dialogue are also excellent choices for shared reading because the different parts are already defined. Taking turns is particularly beneficial when children have difficulty reading their school textbooks. By reading every other paragraph, section, or part, we provide a support system that helps a child understand what is in the text and keep the text going. Occasional pauses to offer comments and ask if the youngster has any questions can help clear up misunderstandings. As the child begins to feel more confident reading independently, we can read less and less of the text. In the meantime, the shared reading is much like a conversation: neither reader is solely responsible for doing the entire reading.

At times children may want to stop to talk about the story, asking questions or clarifying information. When this happens, it provides both readers with an opportunity to share information with one another. When children do stop to ask questions or share information, it's

44 Reading books with children

necessary to keep in mind that they not perceive time spent sharing as test time. Quizzing children on what they have just read could easily discourage them from reading.

Talking about the book at a later time is both enjoyable and beneficial because it helps to reflect on what has just been read. It is a good time to discuss parts of the book that were informative as well as troublesome. While discussing the book, we can help children relate information found in the book to other things they are learning in their lives. This time also helps us become aware of other information we might want to explore with our children.

When children do want to read, it is important others respect their efforts by letting them read without interruption. If children have trouble with some of the words in a story, we can give them a go-ahead signal—a signal that helps them learn that they should not spend too much time trying to pronounce unfamiliar words or trying to find someone else to tell them how to pronounce them. To give children a go-ahead signal, we can tell them to skip a word they may not know and then when they're through reading, if they still want to know what the word is, we will talk about it. When children go on, they usually find that the context helps them figure out what the word was. Thus, they discover for themselves the value in using all of the context to figure out unknown words. When they do that, children have learned an important lesson: they don't have to quit reading a book when they encounter too many unfamiliar words.

If by the time they are finished reading, children have not figured the word out for themselves and still want to know what it is, then we can help them with the troublesome word. An effective thing to do is read a part of the story containing the unfamiliar word. Often when children hear someone else pronounce the word, they recognize what it is. At times it is not the pronunciation that gives children a problem but instead it is the way a word is used in a particular context that is the problem. When children don't understand the meaning of a word in a particular context, we can discuss with them the

Why listen to children read? **45**

intended meaning after they have finished reading. Helping youngsters then can be of more help than interrupting to point the word out while reading, because by reading on, children have more context to use. The main thing to keep in mind is that whenever the reader stops or is interrupted, comprehension usually suffers.

Even if children would like to read on or make substitutions, some children may be afraid to do so for fear of being corrected. Therefore, it is important not to stop a child's reading for the purpose of making a correction. Instead children should be encouraged to read on and make their own corrections.

When I first heard that refraining from correcting was important to a child's growth as an independent reader, I must admit I had difficulty restraining myself. Fortunately, over the years, many readers have convinced me of the wisdom of this tactic: Children can make their own corrections, and the ability to do so is an important part of the reading process. When I find it difficult to refrain from correcting, I try to sit where I can't see what the child is reading. That way I can relax and not worry about what's on the page.

One of the children who helped me understand that children need to make their own corrections was Amy. One day Amy was reading a story that had the following sentence in it: "I have a huge bike." When Amy came to the word *huge*, she stopped and tried several times to sound it out. With each attempt, Amy said something that resembled "hug." Although I was tempted to tell her the word was *huge*, I bit my tongue and waited to see what she would do. Finally, Amy said, "Hug." Even though her voice indicated she was not too satisfied with that pronunciation, she continued reading. As soon as Amy read the word *bike*, though, she said, "Oh, that word is *huge*, isn't it?" I nodded my head yes. Amy grinned and continued reading. Like many readers, Amy did not need to be corrected. What Amy needed was to know she should use upcoming information and let the context of the story help her.

By not interfering while they are reading, we help children become aware that the print yet to come is of help to them. Even within the boundaries of a single

46 Reading books with children

word, the following letter often influences the pronunciation of the preceding letters. For example, Frank Smith (1982), a reading researcher, points out that the pronunciation of *o* in the following words depends upon the letters that follow it: *ho, hot, hotel, hoop,* and *house.*

Another example of what Smith is saying about information to process print often being ahead of the reader can be seen in the following sentence: "I read the newspaper yesterday." To know which of the two pronunciations of *read* to use, either /red/ or /reed/, the reader must read further. Only when encountering the word *yesterday,* does the reader know which pronunciation of *read* to use.

Sometimes children may read on for several pages before recognizing they may have mispronounced, substituted, or omitted a word earlier. When that happens, parents can rejoice at how much the child has been reading for meaning and not just for pronounciation. Even when children do not self-correct, no harm is done. If not knowing a word, making a substitution, or omitting part of the story either interferes with comprehension or intrigues the reader or the listener, the word, or words, can be discussed *after* the story is completed.

By encouraging children to read without interruption, we help them become independent readers. True, a child may not read verbatim and pronounce all the words as the parent would; but when adults step in and assume the reading, they convey a sense of distrust for the child's efforts. They also deny the youngster an opportunity to try reading for himself or herself.

Whenever I think of letting children try out reading for themselves, I'm reminded of an experience a friend had with her oldest granddaughter. Because Elizabeth wanted to get upstairs in a hurry, she carried Joyce instead of letting her walk by herself. Although Joyce squirmed and kicked, Elizabeth managed to hold her. At the same time Joyce kept saying, "I'll do it, I'll do it." When they got to the second floor, Joyce immediately crawled back downstairs and climbed back up. In the process she wobbled a bit but she did make it to the top on her own.

The same is true when children want to read. They want to try doing it themselves, and in the process they may wobble a bit and seem unsteady. Letting children do their own reading helps them gain strength as readers and lets them know we respect their efforts.

Why acquire a personal library?

By having a personal library, children have easy access to a book when they want to entertain themselves or find information they may need. Acquiring books at an early age also helps children build and sustain an interest in books. If your children do not already have a library, you may want to start one now. You can begin by helping them be on the lookout for various kinds of books, such as nursery rhymes, storybooks, books of rhymes and riddles, novels, mysteries, biographies, legends, and joke books. Not to be overlooked are other reading materials such as a globe, maps, posters, magazines, newspapers, and stamp and coin albums.

A good starting place is to check books you may have saved from your own childhood. Oftentimes our children are unaware of interests we had as children. When we share books that we liked, we share a bit of our own childhood with them. If you have saved some books, get them out and place them on your children's bookshelf.

If you want new books, most shopping malls have bookstores in them. You can stop in and get acquainted with the salespeople, who will help you select books and, if necessary, order any they don't have. Because many books come in both hardcover and paperback, you can check for the kind that best fits your children's needs. Also be sure to ask the bookstores to inform you when they are having inventory-reduction sales.

Other sources for buying new books include children's book-of-the-month clubs, which are often available through schools. Each month book companies such as Scholastic send brochures to the schools encouraging children to order books, which are usually inexpensive paperbacks and represent a variety of topics. Many parenting magazines carry advertisements for children's

48 Reading books with children

book-of-the-month clubs. Some of these clubs also have books with accompanying read-along cassettes or records.

To find used books, scout out garage and rummage sales; Goodwill and Salvation Army stores; and community-sponsored book sales, usually held in a park, local bank, or community building. You can also inquire about sales the local library may have. At times libraries cull books that are no longer usable for general circulation but are too good to throw away. Well-used books are a good indication they've been children's favorites. Therefore, they make excellent choices. Additionally, you can ask relatives and friends for any books they talk about disposing. Although you may not be interested in all the books, finding a few special ones can be worth your time and effort.

Another thing you can do is suggest to relatives and friends that books would be a welcome gift for your children. Many people will be happy for that suggestion because books are relatively easy to shop for, especially if you indicate the kinds or titles of books your children are interested in. Also books, particularly paperbacks, can be less expensive than many toys or clothing items, thus, they make a relatively inexpensive gift.

A magazine subscription in a child's name also makes an excellent gift. For several years I've sent a subscription for *National Geographic WORLD*, a magazine published by the National Geographic Society, to some of my young friends. Not only do the children enjoy receiving their own magazine but they also enjoy sharing it with their parents. Thus, the magazine has become one of the many ways my friends and their parents share a common interest with one another.

How can a parent find time?

Given the busy and varied schedules we keep, finding time to read with our children can be a problem for many of us. If that is a concern of yours, the following story may sound familiar.

How to find time? **49**

A couple of years ago after I had discussed with a group of parents the importance of reading to children and listening to them read, one mother spoke up and said, "What you're saying is nice, but how am I supposed to find time to do it? I have a full-time job, and by the time I get home at night I'm so tired and there's still the cooking and other chores to do. I just don't have time to do everything." Having worked outside the home myself, I could empathize with what the mother was saying. Before I could reply though, a mother who worked at home said, "I'd like to respond to that question, if you don't mind."

Mrs. Allen said that at one time she used to think she didn't have any extra time to read to her children either, but she learned to listen to them read while doing other things. She explained that as she stirred the gravy or washed the dishes, her youngsters took turns reading to her. When she finished telling us this, Mrs. Allen paused and then said, "And now that I'm thinking about it, next time I'll read to them while they wash the dishes."

Following Mrs. Allen's response, another parent explained that he helped solve the time problem by making audiocassette tapes whenever he read a new book to his children. Then, when he was either gone or too busy to read to them, they could still listen to him read. When I told a neighbor that idea, she said, "Why didn't I think of using tapes? Mother and I send tapes back and forth all the time so she can hear the kids talking. I'll just ask her to read some stories on the next set."

In addition to recording stories you and other adults read, your children can record stories they read, too. Then when you find a convenient time, you can enjoy listening to your children. If you are fortunate enough to have access to a camcorder or movie camera, you can capture not only your children's voices on tape but also their actions as well. Regardless of the type of equipment you use, in years to come the tapes will provide memories for you and your children.

Reading to and with children need not be limited to parents only. You can ask other children in the family

50 Reading books with children

to read to one another. And whenever grandparents, aunts, uncles, and friends are around, they can be invited to share a book with a youngster.

Those of you who work outside your homes and find it difficult to read to your children, may want to ask individuals who care for them to read to them. If youngsters go to a day-care center or nursery school, you can send some of their favorite books along with them. Having a familiar book to look at or listen to can help a little one bridge the gap between home and other care. Additionally the school will probably appreciate having some familiar books available to read to the children. If preschoolers are cared for at home by a babysitter, you can ask him or her to read sometime during the day.

Even though we often feel we do not have enough time or are too tired, taking a little time to read to our children can be as relaxing for us as it is for them. I can clearly remember the many times when all I wanted to do was rest for a few minutes after working outside my home all day. When there are little kids around the house, we all know that's an impossibility. What I learned to do though was to take a little time with my son, otherwise he fussed for my attention. Reading a book to him, or having him read to me, gave him the attention he wanted and gave me a chance to rest for a minute or two at the same time. From my own experience, I know that spending a few minutes was relaxing for me as well as beneficial to my son.

But when time is limited, you should not feel guilty when you are unable to read to your youngsters. Instead take satisfaction and pleasure in those times that you *can* read with them.

An invitation to explore and reflect

As a means of exploring and reflecting upon reading books with your children, I invite you to read some books with them. While reading, explore what there is about the reading circumstances and about the books that make the experience a memorable one. Among other

An invitation to explore and reflect **51**

things ask yourself if the circumstances generate a sense of warmth and security and provide a time when you can share information with one another. Also ask yourself if the books are effective in helping your children follow the story, chime in, learn new concepts, extend and enhance current knowledge, or tune into the language of books.

As a part of your exploration, you can also ask your children why they like you to read to them as well as why they like to read to you. Be sure to inquire about the kinds of books they like to listen to and the kinds they like to read. Ask them to tell you about their favorite books and what makes them special. Also ask them to share any particularly memorable moments they experienced when you read with one another.

After you have completed your explorations, take time to reflect on what you have learned. To do this, you might want to make a note of the books your children like and reasons why. You might also want to make a record of the books you have found to be particularly good read-aloud books. Then when you and other parents are talking about books your children like, you can share your list. This list can act as one of the other memories you are keeping of your children's growth and will also help your children have a sense of their own reading growth and have a record, later in life, of the books they enjoyed.

Making tapes is a way for you to reflect at a later time, too, and to record memories. As is true of any written records you are keeping, the tapes are a means by which you preserve special moments when reading books with your children.

Although reading with children is important, writing with them is no less so. In chapter 4 I'll talk about the value in writing with children.

WRITING WITH CHILDREN

Writing with children not only provides them with a demonstration of what writers do but also provides us with insight into what children know about writing.

One day when Mike and his mother stopped by to visit, I gave Mike a pencil and some paper and asked him if he would like to write a story. While his mother was protesting that he didn't know how to write, Mike drew a picture. When I asked Mike to write his name on his picture so that I would be sure to remember it was his, he readily complied (see Figure 4–1). His mother was amazed. She was unaware that Mike was learning to write each time he played with his set of magnetic letters, drew in his coloring books, and observed others writing.

Not surprisingly, then, Mike's mother didn't have any idea that Mike could write his name. Although she had encouraged him to play with the magnetic letters and use crayons, she had been reluctant to let him use a pencil for fear he would write incorrectly and, as a result, develop bad writing habits. When I asked her if she had been hesitant about letting Mike talk for fear he would

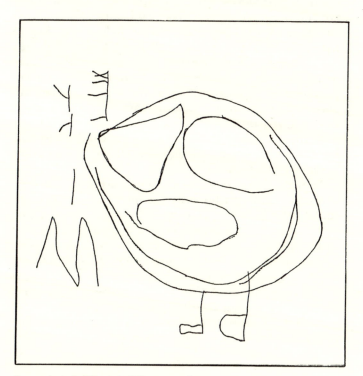

Figure 4–1 Self-Portrait (Mike, age 4)

54 Writing with children

talk incorrectly, she replied, "Of course not." She said the entire family had talked to Mike and encouraged him to respond long before he could say his first words. Each time they fed, bathed, and changed him, Donna and her husband talked to him. They told him how cute he was, how proud they were of him, and what a good baby he was. Then they waited for Mike to respond with a smile or coo. At times, Donna said that Mike even seemed to be talking to them.

When Mike did say his first recognizable word, Donna said she reacted like the typical parent. She could hardly wait to tell everyone Mike had said "Mommy" even though, in reality, what Mike had said sounded more like "Ma-ma."

As Donna continued to talk about what she and others did when Mike was first learning to talk, I suggested that children learn to write in a similar way. Before saying their first words, children experiment with and test out the sounds they can make and want others to pay attention to what they are doing. When learning to write, children experiment with and test out what they can do with a pencil, pen, or crayons and want others to notice what they are doing. Children who are encouraged to explore writing in the same way they are encouraged to explore talking learn to write in much the same way they learn to speak. Fortunately most parents are not afraid to encourage their children to talk. Unfortunately, many parents *are* afraid to encourage their children to write.

Actually, we need not be afraid to encourage children to write. Children who write do not acquire bad habits. Rather, children who write become writers. Encouraging children to write will both heighten their awareness of print and enhance what they already know. And, as we will soon discover, even young children—without anyone to tell them how to hold a pencil, to make the letters of the alphabet, or to spell words—already know much more about writing than we previously thought.

As you no doubt noticed when you explored the language environment of your home, print is everywhere in our society. Children see print not only in books, magazines, and newspapers but also on such things as television; signs; goods in the grocery store; menus; the packages their toys come in; the jars, cans, and boxes their food comes out of; bulletin boards; birthday cakes; mail; and the clothing they wear. And children pay attention to and learn from this print. Even very young children are constantly learning from both the print that surrounds them and their own attempts to produce print. In fact, the two experiences complement one another. Children who write develop a heightened awareness of the print around them. That awareness of their surrounding print environment aids children in their writing. If we have any doubt as to whether or not children learn from these experiences, all we have to do is look at what children do when they write. If we carefully examine what they write, listen to what they say while they are writing, and ask them to tell us about their writing after they finish it, we can begin to discover the tremendous amount of learning that goes on—without any direct instruction—in the lives of very young children.

Why write with children?

Whenever we write with children, we provide them with demonstrations that help them learn from us. We also provide them with a ready audience. In return, children give us insight into the knowledge they have about writing—knowledge we would not be aware of if we didn't write *with* children.

In 1981 Frank Smith made the point that children are surrounded by innumerable demonstrations that help them learn about their world. Most of us provide our children with many demonstrations rather routinely. As part of the normal activities of daily living, we also provide innumerable writing demonstrations. Each time we write letters and cards, attach notes to message boards, and make shopping lists we demonstrate to children what writers do. To illustrate what I mean, let me share the Christmas list Michael wrote (see Fig. 4–2).

56 Writing with children

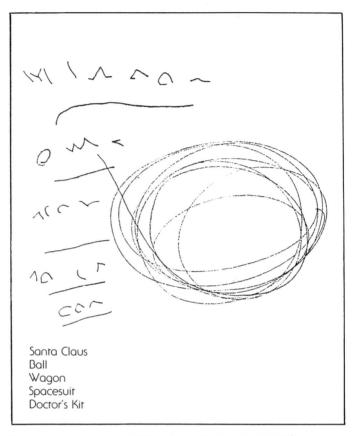

Figure 4–2 Christmas List (Michael, age 3 years 11 months)

Because Michael usually filled the page with print whenever he wrote anything, I was surprised the day he produced only a few lines. When I asked Michael to read what he had written, he pointed to the first line of print, drew a line under it, and said it was Santa's name. Then for each of the other four lines of print, Michael did the same thing while at the same time saying the words *ball, wagon, spacesuit,* and *doctor's kit.* Finally, Michael pointed to the large circular lines and said that was how big he wanted the ball to be. Being curious about the other lines that Michael had drawn, I asked him to tell me

Why write with children? **57**

what they meant. Michael responded that the lines didn't mean anything but his mother puts them on her shopping list. Certainly Michael's mother had provided him with a demonstration each time she wrote her shopping list.

Of course, the most personal writing demonstration available to children is when we include them in writing we do. A few years ago a group of parents and I compiled a booklet listing the various kinds of writing we could do with children while engaged in many of our routine family activities. Our list included writing grocery lists, invitations, and thank-you notes; sending cards for special occasions; filling out order blanks and coupon refund information; writing for information advertised on television or in magazines and newspapers; and labeling photograph, coin, and stamp albums. At a later time, one of the parents called to tell me he had another idea to add to our list. Dan said that prior to taking family trips, he and his family always type a supply of address labels to be used on postcards they want to send to family and friends. He said the highlight of a recent trip was when his two-year-old daughter joined other family members and sent cards to her friends, too.

Recently another one of the parents told me she had extended Dan's idea. Shirley said that whenever her children are on family outings, they write cards not only to others but to themselves as well. When they arrive home, the children not only have mail waiting for them but also have a tangible memory of their trip. Then the first day her children lament they have nothing to do she suggests that they sort the cards and put them into a scrapbook.

In any instance of writing with children we demonstrate what we do as writers and that often we, too, have problems when writing. For example, I often need to restate what I'm saying, to add or change a word, or to rethink the spelling of a word. Such writing behavior on the part of an adult shows children that other writers make changes in their text, rethink what they want to write, and at times have trouble spelling words, too.

Writing with children also helps us gain some insight

58 Writing with children

into what they know about writing; we are able to watch what they do and listen to what they talk about. Both the written message and the talk about that message give us some idea of what children know.

When writing with children, we not only demonstrate literate behaviors but also act as their audience. Like the rest of us, children often have questions while they are writing. They may want to know if what they are writing makes sense. Or they may simply want to share information. As adults, we rely on friends and colleagues to answer our questions and be a sounding board for us. Children, too, need people to respond to their writing. As their audience, we can provide immeasurable support in the learning process by helping them seek answers for themselves and by directing them to other information they may need. Thus, whether we are writing with them or listening to what they've written, by being responsive we can assist children in their attempts at writing.

Often children want to read what they have written because they are proud of what they have done. By listening to them, we recognize children as writers. Often children want us to read what we have written. By listening to us, children extend their knowledge of purposes for writing as well as learn that we often have some of the same problems they have. Adults, too, stop to change a word, cross out something they no longer want, or ask someone to listen to what they're trying to say. When we rewrite and reread what we've written, children see that adults don't always write perfectly the first time either. We, too, learn each time we write.

We also recognize children as writers when we display their work on the refrigerator, in our offices or in other work places, and when we enclose their writing in family letters. Because most children are very anxious to have their work displayed, they willingly supply pictures, notes, and letters. Children who receive responses to letters they have written often want to follow up with a return letter. Thus, a habit of writing letters is begun.

Even though they would like to display their work and write to family members and friends, some children have

Why write with children? **59**

a fear of writing, because they feel their writing is not like that of others. One parent told me that her six-year-old had decided not to write because he was afraid no one could read what he had written. When she suggested he write a letter to Santa Claus, assuring him that Santa can read anything, Tom was less reluctant to write. Tom not only wrote a letter to Santa but enclosed a gift for him, a book he titled *Trks* (*Trucks*).

Tom's concern is not an uncommon one. Once they have more print information and knowledge at their disposal, children recognize that their writing is not like other writing they see around them. Thus, a child who had been an eager writer at an earlier age may seem less eager when older. By accepting their writing, we help children overcome their fears and enhance what they already know.

We can also help children overcome their fears by acting as a support system. Sally, a parent I met several years ago, helped me to understand the importance in offering children a support system. When Doug, her eight-year-old son, was younger, he always enjoyed writing letters to his grandparents who lived in a distant state. But as Doug got older, his grandparents began to comment on his handwriting and any misspelled words. As a consequence, Doug became less and less enthusiastic about writing to them. Sally, appreciating his feelings, suggested they write letters together. Doug's job was to get his thoughts down on paper, and his mother's job was to type his letters. As Doug's fear of writing eased, he gradually began to want to write letters without his mother typing them for him. By being sensitive to her child's feelings, Sally was valuing her son's efforts to write. As a result, not only was Doug beginning to enjoy writing but his mother was finding writing with him a pleasant experience.

Not knowing how to spell a word is a frequent stumbling block for some children. We can help children overcome this problem by giving them a go-ahead signal to keep on writing. One mother, for example, solved the problem of her son continually asking how to spell words. One day, when Jim wanted his mother to buy

60 Writing with children

him a special toy, Jean told him to write it on her shopping list. When Jim insisted he couldn't do that, Jean said, "If you want it, you'll have to write something so I'll know what I'm supposed to buy. Otherwise I can't buy it." Without any further question about whether or not he could write the name of the toy, Jim wrote a reasonable facsimile of the word. Because pictures as well as words can be used to communicate meaning, an extension of Jean's advice to her son is to tell youngsters to draw a picture that will remind them of what they want.

Another go-ahead signal we can give children is to tell them to spell the word the way they think it might be spelled and we'll talk about it later. Telling children to spell the word the best way they can and keep on writing helps them retain a focus on what they are saying. In other words, they don't lose their train of thought. Telling children that we will talk about the word later helps them to know we are not abandoning them. We will help them after they've had a chance to finish writing down their thoughts. Often when continuing to write, children discover the spelling by themselves and thus no longer want our assistance.

One of the things we can do when talking about words children want to know how to spell is tell them to do what many of us do. That is, make a list of possible ways the word could be spelled and then select the one that looks right to them. When children do that, they often recognize the conventional spelling of the word they have been unsure about.

Sharon, a six-year-old, can help us see the wisdom in encouraging children to use their environment to spell words. While writing a story, Sharon asked her mother how to spell the word *alligator*. Because Sharon's mother was talking on the telephone, she told Sharon to wait a minute then she would help. Becoming impatient, Sharon announced to her mother, "I'll find it myself." When her mother finished talking on the phone, Sharon triumphantly announced that she had found the word in one of her books and had spelled it herself.

From Sharon we can learn that it is not always necessary to tell children how to spell a word. Sharon has helped herself learn that she need not always depend upon someone else. Having her mother spell the word may have been convenient for Sharon, but by searching for the word herself, she learns writers need not stop writing when no one is available to spell words they want to use.

At times children are like many of us. They want another writer to verify their spelling. When children ask, "Is that word spelled right?" we can do what we would do with others. We can tell them how we would spell the word, perhaps going to the dictionary for verification. If we are uncertain ourselves about the spelling, we can suggest children seek out someone else. Doing this helps children know that we, too, have problems spelling some words and need to consult other sources.

What to look for in children's writing?

Often when looking at children's writing, particularly the writing of very young children, many people are inclined to think the child has only done some scribbling. But in the past few years many people have discovered that what may appear to be random and careless marks are more than that; they represent a child's endeavors to write (Bean and Bouffler 1987; Clay 1975; Harste, Woodward, and Burke 1984; Hill 1980). By writing with children and listening to what they have to say about their writing, we can discover they, among other things, establish their signatures; discover many letters of the alphabet; try out different scripts; placehold information; write stories, letters, and personal shopping lists; and make logical spelling decisions—all at a very young age.

Several years ago a mother insisted that she knew her four-year-old son, Mark, certainly didn't know anything about writing. To assure Mrs. Taylor that he may know more about writing than she thought, I suggested that she do some writing with him and take particular notice of what he did. Then later we would talk about what she observed. While Mark's mother was writing with her

62 Writing with children

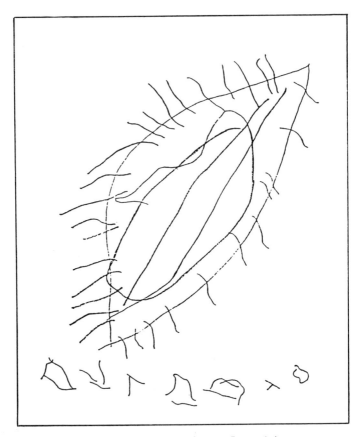

Figure 4–3 Spider Story (Todd, age 2 years 5 months)

older son, I did some writing with Todd, her two-and-a-half-year-old son. As I gave Todd a pencil and some paper, I asked him if he would like to write a story for me. Todd responded by making a large oval shape and adding numerous lines to it (see Figure 4–3). While working, Todd talked about spiders and the many legs they have. Then Todd made what appeared to be a number of random shapes: As he made each shape, Todd whispered the letter names D, T, T, S, and D. When I asked Todd to tell me

What to look for in children's writing? **63**

what he had written, he pointed to the picture and said it was a spider. Then he pointed to the shapes underneath the spider picture and repeated the letter names he had said earlier. Clearly Todd was aware of some of the letters in either his first or last name. Todd was also aware he could tell a story about spiders by drawing a picture. Knowing that Todd's mother would want to observe what he was doing, I beckoned her to join us and suggested that she ask Todd to write his name. As Todd wrote 〒 🖉 and said the names of those two letters, "*T O*," Mrs. Taylor expressed surprise at what her two-and-a-half-year-old son knew. In this instance of writing, Todd helped his mother learn he was establishing his signature.

Wendy, another two-and-a-half-year-old, can also help us learn to look beyond the marks on the paper to discover what children know about writing. After watching a friend of her mother's write, Wendy began to experiment and to explore what she could do with the various Magic Markers Laurie was using. First Wendy picked up one of the markers and made a mark on the paper. Then she did the same thing with each of the other available markers (see Figure 4–4). When she finished trying out all of them, Wendy looked at what she had done, traced her finger over the ∧∨ in the upper right corner, and proudly announced, "Oh, that's a Z like in zebra."

What Wendy did is impressive but not unusual. Beause she could see Laurie making marks on the paper, Wendy wanted to do likewise. Then in the process of making marks, Wendy made one that reminded her of other knowledge she had, knowledge gained from observing the myriad of print in her environment. Although Wendy did not comment about other letters she had formed, notice that she made letters resembling those in her name.

In addition to helping us learn to look more closely at the marks children make while writing, Wendy can also help us learn that we need not force children into writing. Instead providing children with opportunities

64 Writing with children

Figure 4–4 Discovery of a Z (Wendy, age 2 years 6 months)

to play around with markers, pencils, and crayons allows them to make discoveries for themselves.

Having discovered some letters, many children use those letters to generate new letters. An example of a child discovering several letters of the alphabet from a few known letters is Nikki. Recently while I was writing some letters, Nikki wanted to write also. After writing her name, Nikki wrote a number of letters of the alphabet and identified each by name (see Figure 4–5). At first glance, the letters may appear to be random, but they are not. The letters either are letters in Nikki's name or are similar to them.

To appreciate what Nikki has discovered, look closely at the letters she wrote and notice the similarity between those and the letters in her name. By adding a stroke to N, it resembles W or M, or as Nikki wrote a combination of W and M. By adding lines to and subtracting lines

What to look for in children's writing? **65**

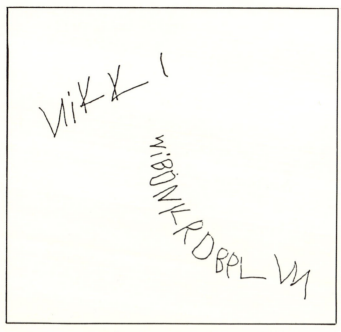

Figure 4–5 Generating a String of Letters (Nikki, age 4 years 9 months)

from *K*, it resembles *B, P, R* or even *L*. And, by removing the inner lines of the *B*, it resembles *D*. Because Nikki has already discovered that letters are similar to one another, we can predict she will eventually discover many other letters.

Nikki did not need me to tell her how to form the letters. She had been learning to do that herself each time she saw those letters in print. Writing with me and others gave her the opportunity to use what she was learning.

Because children often learn the letters in their names first, they frequently use those letters for a variety of purposes. We have seen that children use the letters in their names to establish their signature and to generate other letters. In addition, children often use letters in their name to represent letters and words they sense are

66 Writing with children

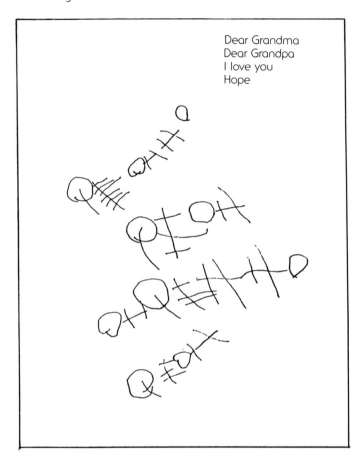

Figure 4–6 Letter to Grandparents (Hope, age 4)

needed. Hope and Alison are examples of this phenomenon.

When looking at children's writing, we can often tell who the writer is because of the letters they choose to use. By looking at Hope's writing shown in Figure 4–6, we can certainly recognize that she has used the letters *H, O, P,* and *E* in a variety of ways. By listening to Hope read what she wrote, we learn she has written a letter to her grandparents. To do that, Hope selected those letters most familiar to her to take the place of letters and

What to look for in children's writing? **67**

Figure 4–7 Letter to Mary (Alison, age 6)

words she has yet to learn. In doing that, we can say she has selected one set of letters to placehold another.

When Alison wrote a letter to me, she used the letter *o* to placehold many of the vowels she sensed should be in words she wanted to use. (See Figure 4–7.) Although Alison's spelling may look strange, the principle underlying what she did is not. Sensing she needed a symbol to represent vowel sounds she heard, Alison selected one

68 Writing with children

letter found in her name to placehold some of those sounds. Thus, the letter *o* stands for the *e* sound in *dear*, the *a* sound in *Mary*, the *i* sound in *Hill*, the *a* sound in *have*, and so on. Notice that instead of using the letter *o* in the word *wrote*, Alison invented a similar looking symbol, *∅*. Although we don't know why Alison invented a new symbol, we can guess that she may have felt the need to distinguish the vowel sound in *wrote*, which is an *o*, from the vowel sound heard in the other words, which she had already represented with an *o* even though there is no *o* in them.

According to the research conducted by Harste, Woodward, and Burke (1984), Hope and Alison's behavior is typical. Most writers placehold information when they write. They use abbreviations and numbers to represent words. They use smiley faces to represent "Have a nice day." They use acronyms to represent such things as the National Aeronautics and Space Administration: NASA. And they use functional spelling to placehold an unknown or uncertain spelling until they can consult a dictionary or friend. Hope and Alison were aware they could placehold writing information. Hope did so by using letters in her name and Alison by using the letter *o* for vowels she sensed needed to be in some of the words.

Another thing that we can look for in children's writing is the different scripts they use. As adults we frequently use more than one script—a flowing cursive script or a neat manuscript style of printing. Children do likewise. To demonstrate that children use more than one script, we can look at a story and a letter that Alison wrote when she was five and a half years old. Although one script is less developed, her writing shows she knows two types of script exist.

In the first example, shown in Figure 4–8, Alison wrote a story similar to the Mother Goose story about the old crooked man who walked a crooked mile. When asked to read her story, Alison read,

> *Once upon a time there was an old crooked house and old crooked man lived in it. He caught a crooked—cat*

What to look for in children's writing? 69

Figure 4–8 Old Crooked House Story (Alison, age 5 years 6 months)

that cooked—that got a, that caught a crooked mouse. They all lived together in a little crooked house.

In the second example, shown in Figure 4–9, Alison has written a letter to her brother, which she read as follows:

Jason. I know you have been worrying about me at school and wondering what—what I've been doing, but I know you won't get mad if I play your number up. And do you know what I did on your first try? I went, ah I got all— all of the pegs in—in two, in two chances. And uhm, I know what it is, it is nice outside so—so—take a good look at—at it. Signed Alison

Although Alison uses printing to write her own name and that of Jason's, she uses a series of connected lines,

70 Writing with children

Figure 4–9 Letter to Jason (Alison, age 5 years 6 months)

as is the style of cursive script, to write a story and a letter. Often this type of script is called scribbling. But I prefer to call it personal cursive, because the term scribbling is often thought to be writing that is done randomly and without care. Alison has not written carelessly but instead has written a meaningful message, and to call it scribbling does her an injustice. In using her

What to look for in children's writing? **71**

own personal script, Alison is much like those of us who use our own personal script to write shopping lists and notes to ourselves. Even though the appearance of the writing may look careless, the intent is not. If we want others to know what our message is, we may need to read it to them. The same is true when children write. They can read to us what they have written. When we encourage children to read what they have written, we are not only indirectly telling them that we recognize them as writers but also providing them with a go-ahead signal to continue writing. Listening to children read is advantageous to us as well. Any time we listen to what they have written we are in a position to learn what they are learning about writing.

By only looking at what Alison had done and not asking her to read it, I would not have known that she had a sense about writing stories and letters. Although Alison's story is short, this piece of writing indicates Alison is developing an understanding of the fact that stories usually have characters in them who encounter particular situations that are resolved at the end. Her letter reflects she has a sense that letters begin with a person's name followed by a message that typically includes a request for information and/or the sharing of information on a particular problem, situation, or experience and that they end with some kind of closing and a signature.

Another child who knows more about writing than meets the eye is Jeannette. When Jeannette handed her father some writing she had done, his first reaction was, "I wonder what Jeannette's been scribbling now!" Before he could comment, though, Jeannette told her dad that she had written the day's temperature report (see Figure 4–10). Upon taking a closer look, John said that his daughter's temperature report did look much like those they saw on television. She had written several short lines that included both numbers and letterlike symbols. What had initially looked like scribbles to John took on a new meaning for him after Jeannette explained what she had done. When we have difficulty figuring out what chil-

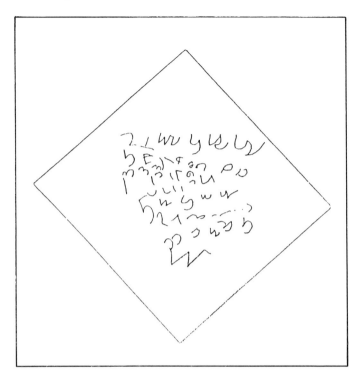

Figure 4–10 Temperature Report (Jeannette, age 4)

dren have written, asking them to read it to us is always a good idea because it gives us more of an insight into what they are attempting to do.

When we look at Scott's writing, we might think that this six-year-old has written only some unrelated letters. But when Scott reads what he wrote, we learn he has written about something that interests him—his pets (see Figure 4–11):

> *The box has kittens.*
> *There are nine kittens.*
> *Kittens are sweet kittens.*
> *The kittens are three months old.*

While writing about his kittens, Scott was working on several aspects of writing. One of the things he was work-

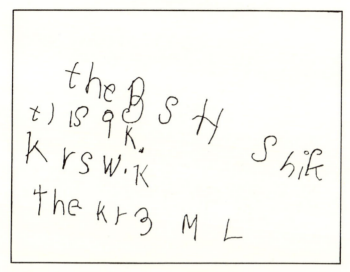

Figure 4–11 The Box of Kittens (Scott, age 6)

ing on was sentence structure. Notice that the last sentence is not nearly as simple and terse as the first three sentences. Another thing he was working on was punctuation. Although he used only one period at the end of a sentence, placing a period within the third sentence is an indication Scott was aware of periods. Having become aware of them, Scott was using them even where not needed. Also, he was working on beginning and ending sounds of words and prominent sounds he heard in some words. To appreciate what he has done, notice the spelling choices he has made for *boxes/bs, has/hs, kittens/k, sweet/sw, months/m* and for *are/r* and *old/l*.

Although Scott was a reluctant writer, we can see in this writing that when writing about something that interested him, he had no problem expressing himself. Therefore, when we encourage children to write, particularly if they are reluctant to do so, we need to keep in mind that children are no different than adults. Children, too, tend to enjoy writing on topics that are familiar and of interest to them.

In spite of the fact that some children's spelling may

74 Writing with children

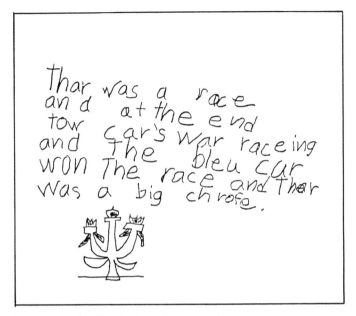

Figure 4–12 The Trophy Story (Jason, age 7)

look strange, most of the time children make logical spelling decisions as illustrated in Scott's writing. To further illustrate this point, I will share a story that Jason, a seven-year-old, wrote. (See Figure 4–12.) Although some of the words Jason has used are not spelled conventionally, most people have no trouble reading his story. A possible exception might be the word *trophy*. The choice of *chr* for *tr* may appear to be haphazard, but it is not. The substitution can be easily explained and, in fact, offers convincing evidence that Jason is on his way to becoming a proficient speller.

The work of Charles Read in the 1970s can help us understand Jason's choice. Read says that because *ch* and *t* are similarly articulated (the tip of the tongue is touching the palette at the back of the upper front teeth), the fact that children often substitute *ch* for *t* clearly illustrates that children do not make haphazard spelling choices. Rather, they make logical and explainable choices.

To test out what Read has discovered, pronounce the

What to look for in children's writing? **75**

words *churn* and *trophy*, pausing briefly at the beginning of each word in order to feel the articulation point for *ch* and *t*. After doing that, I think you will realize that Jason has made a realistic choice to spell *trophy/chrofe*. Children often spell *dress/jres, root/loot,* and *poppy/bobby* or omit letters that are not articulated as in *lamb/lam.* These spellings, too, are consistent with Read's research. They do not illustrate poor spelling. Rather, they illustrate a sophisticated knowledge of spelling.

Jason's seemingly haphazard spelling of the word *trophy* with a final *e* and the word *there* with an *a* can also be explained. According to Read, when a vowel sound coincides with the name of a letter, children will use that letter to represent the sound they hear. For example, because Jason hears the name of the letter *e* and not the name of the letter *y* at the end of *trophy*, his spelling reflects that letter-sound relationship. Alison's spelling (see page 67) of *Mary/More, daddy/dode,* and *story/store* indicates she is aware of that relationship, too. Both children have recognized the close relationship between the name of the letter *e* and the sound they hear at the end of each of the above words.

In spelling *there/thar*, Jason indicated that he recognizes *a* is a closer sound match than *e* is. His choice of *thar* is also similar to the spelling of the rhyming words *hare, care,* and *fare*. Notice that the second time Jason wrote the word *there*, he began by spelling it *thar*. Then he wrote an *e* over the *a*. What Jason did was notable for many reasons. First, Jason was self-editing while writing. Second, Jason was demonstrating that words are not always spelled the way they sound. Third, he was indicating that he was using his visual memory for spelling. And fourth, although Jason's second choice for spelling *there/ther* is not correct, he is moving closer to the expected spelling.

Jason's selection of *two/tow* and *blue/bleu* can also be explained. In spelling *two/tow*, Jason indicated that he was aware that the other two homophones, *to* and *too*, both begin with the letters *to*. Also, the sound heard at the beginning of two is not that found in the majority of words that begin with *tw*. Although Jason probably hasn't studied *tw* words in the English language, if he

76 Writing with children

were to do so, he would find that in most instances when *tw* appears at the beginning of a word, the sound of it is the one found in the words *twin, twist,* and *twenty,* not the sound he is looking for to spell the name of the number between one and three. Jason's choice of *tow* for *two,* therefore, was a reasonable one.

Bleu is a particularly interesting spelling. Although the word has been borrowed from the French, a different spelling for the word is used in the United States. Thus Jason's choice is considered to be incorrect. If Jason were living in France or writing about bleu cheese, he would be correct. What Jason has done is not unusual. Other children (and some adults) have trouble with many words that have been borrowed from other languages. Such words include *theatre/theater, behaviour/behavior,* and *dialogue/dialog.* A friend of mine who lives in England often says that she wishes I would spell *color* correctly. Spelling *color* correctly for her means, of course, spelling it *colour.*

Although in each of the above instances, Jason did not spell the words conventionally, he made some legitimate decisions about spelling. He made those decisions based on how a word is articulated—*trophy/chrofe;* how closely a letter resembles the name of a letter—*there/thar;* how closely a word resembles another word—*two/tow;* and how a word looks in another context—*blue/bleu.* Because of the spelling decisions Jason has made, we can be assured he is a better speller than one might think he is. With continued opportunities to write and read, Jason's sensitivity to spelling will be further enhanced.

Other evidence of Jason's growth as a writer abounds in this piece. For example, his use of the apostrophe in *car's* is an example of an overgeneralized use of a punctuation mark. Children typically will overgeneralize the use of periods, quotation marks, exclamation points, and apostrophes. Having noticed that other writers use such marks, children will use them at every opportunity, whether needed or not. They begin sentences with periods, put periods at the end of lines, end sentences with exclamation marks, and add an apostrophe to words ending with *s.* Thus, a child's latest discovery often shows up in future writing.

What to look for in children's writing? **77**

Figure 4–13 Note to Mary (Chris, age 6)

Chris, a six-year-old, showed he knew something about writing notes for special reasons. A few years ago I had just moved into a new community and Chris, one of my new neighbors, sensing I was a bit lonely, left a note at my front door (see Figure 4–13). In addition to learning an important social amenity, Chris was discovering that notes usually consist of a short message, often including a picture. Chris included both in his note.

What all of these children can help us learn is that children—even very young children—know more about writing than we've previously thought. They know writing serves many functions, including writing stories and letters. They have become aware of salient characteristics of letters of the alphabet, different scripts, and the structure writing takes in stories and letters. And they make logical spelling decisions.

What to provide in a writing place?

Providing a writing place need not be a major financial investment. Having a desk and special writing instruments may be desirable, but it is not necessary. My experience is that most children, even if they have their own desk, like to write in the midst of other people, using whatever pen or pencil they can find. Often the best desk in most homes is the kitchen or dining-room table. The mother mentioned earlier, who devised a writing place for her daughters by placing a table leaf across the arms of a large chair, gave her daughters a place to write that also enabled other family members to be close enough to answer questions and to enjoy watching what the girls were doing.

Because young children, in particular, seem to have an insatiable desire to write, we can keep them from writing on the walls by providing other things for them to write on. A friend told me that she hangs a large piece of wrapping paper on one of her kitchen doors for the family to write on. When she first started doing that, Gloria's intention was that the paper would be something for her preschoolers to write on rather than the walls. Eventually, though, others in the family began to add notes and pictures. Now they have a series of family murals. Other things children can write on, rather than the wall, are chalkboards, magnetic-letter boards, and magic slates.

Unless your children need it for a particular reason, there is no need to buy special lined paper for them. Children can easily write on unlined paper and often prefer it because they feel less restricted. Good sources of paper include old stationery, the back of unsolicited mail, paper bags or wrapping paper, and used computer paper. For easy accessibility, these materials can be placed in a cabinet drawer within children's reach.

When children want to write special letters, they enjoy having their own stationery. A nice gift, therefore, is an assortment of paper or stationery. Other gift ideas include address books, diaries, and autograph books.

Just as you do not need to buy special paper, you do

An invitation to explore and reflect **79**

not need to buy special pencils and crayons for your children either. Even very young children can use the same pencils, pens, crayons, and markers others in the family use. In order for your children to have easy access to a pencil or crayons, you can help them make containers for writing utensils by using any small box and decorating it. Crayons, particularly broken ones, can be kept in margarine tubs. Because there is something special about having a new pen, pencil, or box of crayons, they, too, make good gifts. A particularly personal gift is a pen or pencil with the child's name on it.

Not to be overlooked in a writing spot are books. By having books in the area, you and your children will have easy access to information you may need or can use when writing. Many of the books, particularly the reference books, that you help your children acquire for their personal library will serve as writing resources, too.

Of course the main ingredients for a writing place will be you and your children. Whatever your family situation may be, the time you spend writing together will be a time when you can learn from one another while sharing special moments.

An invitation to explore and reflect

As a means of exploring and reflecting upon writing with your children, I invite you to do some writing with them. To do that, you might want to include them when you write your grocery list, send a letter to family or friends, or fill out an order blank. While writing with your youngsters make a mental note of anything they do and say. Also make a mental note of any directions you give and reactions you have during this experience. These notes will help you reflect on what your children are doing and what you are learning. After you are through writing take time to look closely at what you've done. Notice what your children know about writing and what demonstrations you offered one another.

When observing your children, be sure to focus on what they are learning rather than on what they have yet to learn. Remember, your children are just taking

80 Writing with children

their first steps into the world of writing and cannot be expected to write like adults anymore than they can be expected to talk like adults. Remember, too, that the examples I have shared are intended to be representative of what you can look for in children's writing. You may notice quite different things about your own children's writing. The main thing to keep in mind is that no two children will write exactly alike anymore than they walk or talk alike. Therefore, be sure to look for what *your* children know, and I think you may find they know more about writing than meets the eye.

After you have completed your exploration, take time to reflect upon what you are learning. To do that, I suggest you write about the observations you made. Doing this will provide you with a tangible record of your explorations along with the pieces of writing your children did.

If you have not already been saving some of your children's writing, this experience can be the start of doing so. Keeping their writing, or at least some of it, will provide you with a record of their writing growth. I find it helpful to put a note on the back of the paper indicating the date and any special things I want to remember about the circumstances under which the writing occurred. I also like to make a note of anything the youngster said. This information then helps me to recall at a later time what I've learned from children.

Because school is an extension of the learning environment already created at home, in chapter 5 I will say a word about the family partnership continuing and expanding when children go to school.

5

GOING TO SCHOOL

a continuation and expansion of the family partnership

The knowledge children acquire at home is the basis for the more formal learning they will encounter in school.

When children go to school, they have already been in a highly successful learning environment. Before the age of six, most children can carry on conversations, ask and respond to questions, follow directions, give orders, or share information. They can point out signs on fast-food restaurants, identify channel numbers on a television set, read an often-heard story, or write their own shopping lists. They can pound nails, make mud pies, or play doctor. And they can dress and feed themselves, follow the rules of a game, identify the car their parents drive, or tell how old they are, even holding up the appropriate number of fingers to prove it. In sum, children acquire a vast amount of knowledge in an unbelievably short period of time while in close association with their parents. Then when children go to school, they take this knowledge with them.

Continuing the family partnership

The family partnership children have been engaged in since they were born takes on an added dimension when children go to school. Conversations tend to revolve around school activities; work includes special school projects; and recreation involves school events such as ball games, musical performances, science and young authors' fairs, art shows, and school plays.

The first of many conversations focusing on school usually occurs several months before children go to kindergarten or first grade. Well in advance of the first day of school we discuss a variety of topics concerning it: who their teacher will be, what they will learn in school, how they will get to school, how they should behave, or what supplies they will need. Each instance of talking about school helps children have some expectations before they arrive on the first day. When we talk about school—just as when we talk about a book before reading it—we offer them a preview. Having this preview, then, makes school less foreign to children.

Having a preview also helps children make the transition from home to school as illustrated by the story a colleague shared. Brian said he and his six-year-old daughter recently took a scouting expedition to discover the safest route for Ruth to take whenever walking alone

84 Going to school

to school. While on their walk, they counted the number of main streets Ruth would cross and they stopped to get acquainted with the crossing guards. Brian also gave Ruth instructions about being very cautious when crossing streets without guards. By taking this walk and talking about what she could expect, Brian was helping Ruth to be less apprehensive about walking to school alone. In doing this, Brian had done what many parents do when their children take a first step out of the home learning environment and into another one. He was helping his daughter form a bridge between home and school. Brian, incidentally, was also helping himself form that same bridge.

To answer some of the questions children have, many parents plan a special family outing and take them to meet their teachers and tour the classrooms. This outing helps both the parent and child get acquainted with what will be a new experience in both their lives. It also helps children form a mental picture of school. Then when they hear others talk about it children can visualize the environment.

Another outing many parents take children on is a shopping trip to buy school supplies. Even though children may have paper, pencils, or crayons at home, most parents purchase new ones especially for school. Providing them with some of the tools they will need in school is another way we demonstrate to children our continued interest in their learning.

One of the ways children solicit our participation in their school learning is by asking us for help with their homework. Most of us respond by sharing what we know. We help them figure out written directions; solve math problems; do science experiments; write poems, stories, or research papers; draw maps; or go to the library with them to obtain information they need. If reading textbooks is a stumbling block for them, many of us help children by doing some of the things mentioned in chapter 3, such as helping children read pictures, charts, graphs, and other aids; sharing the reading with them; reading the material to them; or discussing unfamiliar concepts with them.

Continuing the family partnership **85**

Helping children with school work not only gives us an opportunity to share knowledge we have but it also gives us some insight into the things they are learning at school. When we are aware of what they are studying, many of us pick up books and other materials—posters, pictures, brochures, maps, rocks, shells—that can enhance and extend information they encounter. In addition to enjoying these materials at home, many children like to take them to school and share them with their classmates and teachers. Taking these materials to school is an indication they realize resources from home can also serve as resources for school activities. This realization is important because it is one of the ways children make the connection between home and school.

On nights when they don't have school work or finish it early, most children enjoy doing what other family members are doing. Thus, the family activities, mentioned in chapter 1, continue to be a significant part of children's lives. In fact, once children are in school, many of their family activities become more meaningful to them because they can relate what they do at home with what they do in school and vice versa. For example, children who have made change and bought property when playing Monopoly know something about mathematics. Then when they encounter adding, subtracting, multiplying, and dividing in school, those concepts mean more to them. The reverse also happens. Children who experiment with color changes in the science lab by mixing blue and yellow dye together have an understanding of what vegetable coloring to use when wanting green icing on a birthday cake. Having learned a principle in school, they then apply it at home.

Another way to continue the family partnership is by working on projects at home that may relate to things children are doing in school. One mother, for example, spent several weeks working with her two sons coauthoring a book about sea life on the nights the boys had no school work. They began by getting some books from the library. Then the three of them read for information they wanted to include in their book. After getting the necessary information, the mother and her third-grade

86 Going to school

son wrote the text while her fifth-grade son drew pictures to accompany it. When they finished writing their book, they made a copy to present to the school library. Cindy said that the experience was a rewarding one because the three of them shared a special time together, produced a book others could enjoy, and learned more about some concepts the boys were studying in school. As a result of this experience, each of the boys later wrote a book for the young authors' fair their school was sponsoring.

Cindy's experience illustrates that projects done at home are similar to school activities. This is certainly true of extracurricular activities. For example, children who play ball in school usually have been playing ball with a family member or two long before becoming a member of the school team. For many boys and girls, making the team begins with an interested mother, father, or other willing player tossing a ball back and forth to them. Once children make the school team, parents may act as coach, particularly when a school can't afford to hire one. Even when they don't coach formally, parents continue to be involved. They give pointers while practicing with their daughters and sons and make a special effort to provide transportation to the games. Oftentimes family schedules revolve around the team schedule as well—another indication the family partnership has continued.

The extracurricular activities are not limited to sports. They may also include band concerts, dance performances, or art shows. In each of these activities, the home is where the activity frequently started. Parents either taught their children themselves or hired someone to teach them to play an instrument, to learn ballet, or to work with watercolors or other art materials.

As we can see, even though children spend several hours a day at school, the family partnership continues at home. Each time children and their parents discuss the latest school news, work on a science experiment, share a book, talk about a math problem, write a story, or practice shooting baskets they continue to share unique learning moments. These unique learning mo-

Expanding the family partnership **87**

ments at home, therefore, complement the unique learning moments children experience at school and elsewhere.

Expanding the family partnership

Not only does the family partnership continue when our children go to school, but it also expands each time we play a part in school activities. Some of those activities include attending parent-teacher conferences; volunteering to share our talents and expertise in the classroom, library, cafeteria, or office; or assisting with field trips, plays, and athletic events.

Because the teacher plays an important role in children's lives, most schools plan orientation days to introduce teachers—particularly kindergarten and first-grade teachers—to their new students and parents. At this first meeting the teacher talks about some of the things the children will do during the year, provides general guidelines about the school, asks parents to share information, or asks for questions. This visit helps parents to get acquainted with the teacher and the other parents, to have some idea of the forthcoming school year, and to set a tone for the year.

Schools usually schedule other parent-teacher conferences during the year. As a rule these conferences include only the parent and the teacher. But taking children to these conferences can be worthwhile as a friend discovered. Sally said that before she began taking her eight-year-old son to conferences, he worried the entire time she was gone. He was always afraid his mother and his teacher were saying something negative about him. When Sally got home, Don quizzed her about what they had said. Even though reports on him were positive, Don was never quite convinced his mother was being honest with him. When Sally started taking Don to the conferences, everything changed. He heard firsthand what his teacher and his mother had to say about him, and he didn't have to wait for his mother to relay word about his work or behavior. He could hear it for himself. By taking her son to the conference, Sally

88 Going to school

helped him become a partner in the discussion about his own learning.

There is real value in having children present at a conference. During the conference children can show their parents around the classroom and share work they have done. In doing this, they give their parents a glimpse of that learning environment called school. When teachers are included in this sharing as well, they often have an insight into their student's learning they may not have seen before. It is important to make sure everyone has a chance to learn from one another during the conference.

In addition to including children in on conferences, we can do some other things that make conferencing beneficial. Because everyone has busy schedules, going prepared to a conference can be productive without consuming an inordinate amount of time. To prepare for a conference one of the things we can do is to talk with our children about things they would like us to discuss. Making a note of any information we or our children want to share is helpful. That way we don't overlook anything.

In order that everyone sees conferencing as an ongoing process and not just something that happens because it is scheduled on the calendar or because of some emergency, conferences can be scheduled from one to the next. Although most are held at school, having a conference at home can be helpful to parents who are unable to go to the school. Conferences held at home can also be helpful to teachers. In the informal learning environment of the home, teachers can learn about some of the things that interest parents and children. On occasion teachers discover parents have a special talent or expertise. Such a discovery can become the foundation for planning a time when those talents and skills can be shared with children at school.

At times some of us do not think we have much talent or any expertise to share with others. But most of us have more than meets the eye. Rose, the mother who didn't think of herself as a partner in her daughter's literacy development, discovered she could help children

Expanding the family partnership **89**

learn a new skill the day she offered to show some sec-
ond-graders how to quilt. Although Rose thought she
had limited skills to share—primarily because of thinking
she was illiterate—she made beautiful quilts. When her
daughter's teacher prevailed upon her to come to the
classroom to show the children how to quilt, Rose finally
consented. By sharing her talents, Rose not only helped
a group of children learn a new skill but also helped
herself realize she had a skill to share.

Parents who may not have thought of how much teaching they actually do often come to realize it when sharing
a talent or expertise in their children's classroom. Several
years ago, the mother of a third-grader made such a
discovery. While Clare was working with me on plans
for a class field trip, she mentioned that she had always
wanted to teach but didn't think she had any talent for
doing so. When I assured Clare that any mother of three
girls certainly had some talent for teaching, she accepted
my invitation to come into the classroom for a day or
two. Clare found the experience very rewarding and
continued to come each morning for the balance of the
school year. She read to children, listened to them read,
or accompanied them to the library. This experience
helped me, as a teacher, learn that sometimes parents
need a little encouragement to work with children in the
classroom.

If you have been reluctant to work in your children's
classrooms, as Clare was, don't be. Not only will you help
children learn, they will help you learn, because no one
can work with children without learning from them and
about them. If you are reluctant to work in your own
children's classroom, don't dismiss the idea of working
in another classroom as well as in the library, office, or
cafeteria. Working either directly or indirectly with your
children helps both of you appreciate that the learning
partnership expands into the school.

Because many teachers are often unaware of talents
and expertise their students' parents have, developing a
directory for them can be useful. Jennifer, a mother who
had small children at home and was unable to work in
the classroom, assembled such a directory for her daugh-

90 Going to school

ter's teacher. She made a list of the parents' names; telephone numbers; and a brief description of any work, hobbies, and other talents they were willing to share. As she compiled the booklet, Jennifer discovered the parents represented a rich source of experts to call upon —upholsterers, dentists, secretaries, bakers, artists, homemakers, firefighters, nurses, storytellers, musicians, gardeners, and state troopers. This booklet, then, was a ready reference for her daughter's teacher whenever she wanted parents to be guest teachers in the classroom. Because many children are often not aware of their parents' work, an added advantage of parents sharing their expertise is that it helps their own children have a better idea of what they do all day or night. Even children whose parents work at home are often not aware of all that they do there.

At a later time Jennifer extended the directory to include information about parents who had lived in different parts of the world. This proved to be beneficial, too, because a number of parents were willing to share something about their homeland. For example, a mother from Japan showed the children how to do origami; a father from Haiti helped them cook chicken using some unfamiliar spices; and a mother from India demonstrated how to wear a sari. In this role, the parents were the resource experts in the classroom and as such were able to tell the children firsthand about countries they might only read about in books or hear about secondhand from someone else.

Helping to plan and assist with field trips, school plays, and athletic events is a way we can be a participant in the social life of the school. Because of the diversity of these events and the times at which they are held, most of us can select the activity that suits our interests and our family schedule. As is true of other things we do when involved in our children's school lives, taking part in these activities helps everyone learn that school is a continuation of the learning begun at home.

An invitation to explore and reflect

As a means of exploring and reflecting upon the ways you continue and expand upon your family partnership,

An invitation to explore and reflect **91**

I invite you to think of the many school activities you engage in either directly or indirectly. To do that, consider conversations you and your children have about school, the school projects you work on, the extracurricular activities you help plan or assist with, the conferences you and your children attend, and any talents or expertise you have shared at school.

Next select one activity and observe what you learned. For example, you might want to coauthor a book with your children as Cindy did or go to your child's classroom and demonstrate a talent as Rose did. Another thing you might want to do is help with a school project, such as working on a science principle your youngster is studying. While engaged in the activity, notice what you are doing that is continuing or expanding the family partnership.

To reflect on what you have learned, record your thoughts. I think you will agree that what children learn at home supports all the other learning they do in school. I think you will also agree that not only do reading and writing begin at home but they continue to develop there. And, finally, I think you will agree that the role you play in your children's learning, including literacy, is a significant one.

starter list
of
read-aloud
books and
magazines

Books that can be read in a short time

Aardema, Verna. 1975. *Why Mosquitoes Buzz in People's Ears*. New York: Dial.

Arkhurst, Joyce Cooper. 1972. *More Adventures of Spider*. New York: Scholastic.

Barchas, Sarah E. 1975. *I Was Walking Down the Road*. New York: Scholastic.

Becker, John. 1973. *Seven Little Rabbits*. New York: Scholastic.

Bonne, Rose, and Alan Mills. 1961. *I Know an Old Lady*. New York: Rand McNally.

Brown, Marcia. 1947. *Stone Soup*. New York: Scribner.

———. 1957. *The Three Billy Goats Gruff*. New York: Harcourt.

Brown, Hargaret Wise. 1947. *Goodnight Moon*. New York: Harper and Row.

Carle, Eric. 1969. *The Very Hungry Caterpillar*. Cleveland, O.H.: Collins World.

Charlip, Remy. 1969. *What Good Luck! What Bad Luck!* New York: Scholastic.

de Angeli, Marguerite. 1954. *Book of Nursery and Mother Goose Rhymes*. New York: Doubleday.

de Regniers, Beatrice Schenk. 1970. *Catch a Little Fox*. New York: Seabury.

———. 1985. *Jack and the Beanstalk*. New York: Atheneum.

Elting, Mary, and Michael Folsom. 1980. *Q is for Duck*. New York: Clarion Books.

Galdone, Paul, 1968. *Henny Penny*. New York: Scholastic.

———. 1970. *The Three Little Pigs*. New York: Seabury.

———. 1972. *The Three Bears*. New York: Scholastic.

———. 1973. *The Little Red Hen*. New York: Scholastic.

———. 1975. *The Gingerbread Boy*. New York: Seabury.

Geisel, Theodor S. 1957. *The Cat in the Hat*. New York: Random.

Goss, Janet L., and Jerome C. Harste. 1981. *It Didn't Frighten Me!* Worthington, O.H.: Willowisp.

Harste, Jerome C., and Carolyn L. Burke. 1983. *Animal Babies*. Worthington, O.H.: Willowisp.

Hazel, Beth, and Jerome C. Harste. 1982. *My Icky Picky Sister*. Worthington, O.H.: Willowisp.

94 Starter list of read-aloud books and magazines

Heller, Ruth. 1981. *Chickens Aren't the Only Ones.* New
   York: Grosset & Dunlap.
Kraus, Robert. 1972. *Milton the Early Riser.* New York:
   Windmill and Dutton.
Krauss, Ruth. 1945. *The Carrot Seed.* New York: Harper
   and Row.
Lear, Edward. 1983. *The Owl and the Pussy Cat.* New York:
   Holiday House.
McGovern, Ann. 1967. *Too Much Noise.* New York:
   Scholastic.
Moore, Clement. 1980. *The Night Before Christmas.* New
   York: Holiday House.
Parish, Peggy. 1970. *Amelia Bedelia.* New York:
   Scholastic.
Preston, Edna M. 1978. *Where Did My Mother Go?* New
   York: Four Winds.
Rey, H. A. 1941. *Curious George.* Boston: Houghton.
Sendak, Maurice. 1962. *Chicken Soup with Rice.* New
   York: Harper and Row.
———. 1963. *Where the Wild Things Are.* New York:
   Scholastic.
Thomas, Sharon, and Marjorie Siegal. 1982. *No Baths
   for Tabitha.* Worthington, O.H.: School Book Fairs.
Tolstoy, Alexei. 1968. *The Great Big Enormous Turnip.*
   New York: Franklin Watts.
Viorst, Judith. 1972. *Alexander and the Terrible, Horrible,
   No Good, Very Bad Day.* New York: Atheneum.

Books that can be read over a period of time

Blume, Judy. 1976. *Tales of a Fourth-Grade Nothing.*
   New York: Dell.
Cleary, Beverly. 1982. *Ramona the Pest.* New York:
   Dell.
Cohen, Barbara. 1974. *Thank You, Jackie Robinson.* New
   York: Lothrop.
Dodge, Mary Mapes. 1932. *Hans Brinker or The Silver
   Skates.* Garden City, N.Y.: Garden City Publishing.

Starter list of read-aloud books and magazines **95**

Farley, Walter. 1944. *The Black Stallion.* New York: Random.

Fitzhugh, Louise. 1964. *Harriet the Spy.* New York: Dell.

Gipson, Fred. 1956. *Ole Yeller.* New York: Harper and Row.

Lewis, C. S. 1951. *The Lion, the Witch and the Wardrobe.* New York: Macmillan.

Lindgren, Astrid. 1950. *Pippi Longstocking.* New York: Viking.

London, Jack. 1970. *The Call of the Wild.* New York: Scholastic.

O'Brien, Robert C. 1971. *Mrs. Frisby and the Rats of Nimh.* New York: Atheneum.

Paterson, Katherine. 1979. *Bridge to Terabithia.* New York: Avon.

Rawl, Wilson. 1974. *Where the Red Fern Grows.* New York: Bantam.

Sobol, Donald J. 1963. *Encyclopedia Brown, Boy Detective.* New York: Bantam.

Taylor, Mildred D. 1976. *Roll of Thunder, Hear My Cry.* New York: Bantam.

White, E. B. 1952. *Charlotte's Web.* New York: Dell.

Wilder, Laura Ingalls. 1953. *Little House on the Prairie.* New York: Harper and Row.

Wordless picture books

Alexander, Martha. 1970. *Bobo's Dream.* New York: Dial.

Anno, Mitsumasa. 1978. *Anno's Journey.* New York: Philomel.

————. 1982. *Anno's Britain.* New York: Philomel.

————. 1983. *Anno's U.S.A.* New York: Philomel.

dePaola, Tomie. 1979. *Pancakes for Breakfast.* New York: Harcourt Brace.

Goodall, John S. 1969. *The Adventures of Paddy Pork.* New York: Harcourt Brace.

————. 1978. *The Story of an English Village.* New York: Atheneum.

96 Starter list of read-aloud books and magazines

Hogrogian, Nonny. 1972. *Apples*. New York: Macmillan.
Mayer, Mercer. 1967. *A Boy, A Dog and a Frog*. New York: Dial.
Spier, Peter, 1982. *Noah's Ark*. New York: Doubleday.
Turkle, Brinton. 1976. *Deep in the Forest*. New York: Dutton.
Ward, Lynd. 1973. *The Silver Pony*. Boston: Houghton.
Winter, Paula. 1976. *The Bear and the Fly*. New York: Crown.

Children's magazines

Children's Digest. Indianapolis, I.N.: Parents Magazine Enterprises.
Cricket. La Salle, I.L.: Open Court Publishing.
Highlights for Children. Columbus, O.H.: Highlights for Children.
National Geographic World. Washington, D.C.: National Geographic Society.
Owl. Buffalo, N.Y.: National Audubon Society and Owl Magazine.
Sesame Street. New York: Children's Television Workshop.
Zoo Books. San Diego, C.A.: Wildlife Education Ltd.

bibliography

Baghban, Marcia. 1984. *Our Daughter Learns to Read And Write*. Newark, D.E.: International Reading Association.

Barton, Bob. 1986. *Tell Me Another*. Markham, Ontario: Pembroke. Distributed in the U.S. by Heinemann.

Bean, Wendy, and Bouffler, Chrystine. 1987. *SPELL BY WRITING*. Rozelle NSW, Australia: Australian Print Group.

Bissex, Glenda. 1980. *GNYS AT WRK: A Child Learns to Write and Read*. Cambridge, M.A.: Harvard University Press.

Bruner, Jerome S. 1974. "The Ontogenesis of Speech Acts." *Journal of Child Language*, 2:1–19.

Butler, Dorothy. 1980. *Cushla and Her Books*. Boston: Horn Book.

————. 1982. *Babies Need Books*. New York: Atheneum.

Clark, Margart M. 1976. *Young Fluent Readers*. Portsmouth, N.H.: Heinemann.

Clay, Marie M. 1975. *What Did I Write?* Portsmouth, N.H.: Heinemann.

Doake, David B. 1988. *Reading Begins at Birth*. Richmond Hill, ON: Scholastic-TAB Publications. Available in the U.S. from Scholastic Inc.

Evans, David. 1978. *Sharing Sounds*. New York: Longman.

Garnica, O. K. 1975. "How Children Learn to Talk." *Theory into Practice*, 14(5): 299–305.

Gentry, J. Richard. 1987. *Spel. . .Is a Four-Letter Word*. Richmond Hill, ON: Scholastic-TAB Publications. Available in the U.S. from Heinemann.

Goodsell, W. 1915. *A History of the Family as a Social and Educational Institution*. New York: Macmillan.

Harste, Jerome C.; Woodward, Virginia A.; and Burke, Carolyn L. 1984. *Language Stories & Literacy Lessons*. Portsmouth, N.H.: Heinemann.

Hill, Mary W. 1980. "Preschoolers' Print Awareness: An In-depth Study of Three- and Four-Year-Old Children." In *Perspectives on Reading Research and Instruction*, ed. by Michael L. Kamil. Twenty-Ninth Yearbook of the National Reading Conference.

100 Bibliography

Washington, D.C.: The National Reading Conference.

Hodgkin, R. A. 1985. *Playing and Exploring*. New York: Methuen.

Huey, Edmund Burke. 1968. *The Psychology and Pedagogy of Reading*. Reprint. Cambridge, M.A.: M. I. T. Press. Originally published by Macmillan, 1908.

Larrick, Nancy. 1982. *A Parent's Guide to Children's Reading*. 5th ed. New York: Bantam.

Leichter, Hope Jensen, ed. 1974. *The Family as Educator*. New York: Teacher's College Press, Columbia University.

Leichter, Hope Jensen. 1984. "Families As Environments For Literacy." In *Awakening to Literacy*, ed. by Hillel Goelman, Antoinette Oberg, and Frank Smith. Portsmouth, N.H.: Heinemann.

Lindskoog, John, and Lindskoog, Kay. 1978. *How to Grow a Young Reader*. Elgin, I.L.: David C. Cook.

Linkletter, Art. 1957. *Kids Say the Darndest Things*. Englewood Cliffs, N. J.: Prentice.

Martin, Bill, Jr. 1966. *Sounds of Language Readers*. New York: Holt, Rinehart and Winston.

Meek, Margaret. 1982. *Learning to Read*. London: Bodley Head. Distributed in the U.S. by Heinemann.

Newman, Judith. 1984. *The Craft of Children's Writing*. Richmond Hill, ON: Scholastic-TAB Publications. Available in the U.S. from Heinemann.

Pestalozzi, J. H. 1898. *How Gertrude Teaches Her Children*. Syracuse, N.Y.: Bardeen.

Read, Charles. 1975. *Children's Categorization of Speech Sounds in English*. Technical Report No. 197, National Council of Teachers of English, Committee on Research. Urbana, I.L.: NCTE.

Rhodes, Lynn K. 1981. "I Can Read! Predictable Books As Resources for Reading and Writing Instruction." *The Reading Teacher*, 34(5): 511–518.

Rhodes, Lynn K., and Hill, Mary W. 1985. "Supporting Reading in the Home—Naturally: Selected Materials for Parents." *The Reading Teacher*, 38(7): 619–623.

Smith, Frank. 1980. "The Language Arts and the

Learner's Mind." In *Reading Comprehension: Resource Guide*, ed. by B. P. Farr and D. J. Strickler. Bloomington, I.N.: Indiana University Reading Programs.

————. 1981. "Demonstrations, Engagement and Sensitivity: A Revised Approach to Language Learning." *Language Arts*, 52:103–112.

————. 1982. *Understanding Reading*. 3rd ed. New York: Holt, Rinehart and Winston.

Stein, Nancy. 1978. *Children Understand Stories: A Developmental Analysis*. Technical Report No. 69. Urbana, I.L.: University of Illinois, Center for the Study of Reading.

Taylor, Denny. 1983. *Family Literacy: Young Children Learning to Read and Write*. Portsmouth, N.H.: Heinemann.

Taylor, Denny, and Strickland, Dorothy S. 1986. *Family Storybook Reading*. Portsmouth, N. H.: Heinemann. Available in Canada from Scholastic-TAB.

Tough, Joan. 1976. *Listening to Children Talking*. London: Ward Lock. Distributed in the U.S. by Heinemann.

Trelease, Jim. 1982. *The Read-Aloud Handbook*. New York: Penguin.

White, Dorothy. 1984. *Books Before Five*. Portsmouth, N. H.: Heinemann.